THE EMPTY THRONE

Reflections on the History and Future of the Orthodox Episcopacy

LAWRENCE R. FARLEY

ANCIENT FAITH PUBLISHING
CHESTERTON, INDIANA

The Empty Throne: Reflections on the History and Future of the Orthodox Episcopacy
Copyright © 2016 by Lawrence R. Farley

All rights reserved. No part of this publication may be reproduced by any means, electronic, mechanical, photocopying, recording, scanning, or otherwise, without the prior written permission of the Publisher.

Published by:
  Ancient Faith Publishing
  A Division of Ancient Faith Ministries
  P.O. Box 748
  Chesterton, IN 46304
  store.ancientfaith.com

ISBN: 978-1-936270-61-3

Printed in the United States of America

*Dedicated to
my father,
Rheal O. Farley*

"Only love is left"

Contents

Foreword — 7

INTRODUCTION
The Empty Throne: *The Episcopate in Today's Church* — 9

CHAPTER 1
The Bishop in the First Century: *The Hidden President* — 17

CHAPTER 2
The Bishop in the Pre-Nicene Church:
The Voice at the Altar — 35

CHAPTER 3
The Change in the Fourth Century: *An Emerging Elite* — 61

CHAPTER 4
The Bishop in the Fourth Century:
The Patron of the City — 87

CHAPTER 5
The Bishop in Byzantium & Beyond:
The Imperial Monk — 107

CHAPTER 6
The Bishop in the New World: *The Important Visitor* — 125

PRACTICAL CONCLUSIONS: *Filling the Empty Throne* — 143

For Further Reading — 151

Obey your leaders
and submit to them,
for they keep watch
over your souls,
as those who will
give an account.

—HEBREWS 13:17

Foreword

BISHOPS, OR IN A MORE ABSTRACT USAGE, "the episcopacy," comprise that aspect of the Church which has historically been deemed to be the guarantee of ecclesial genuineness. The episcopacy has long been considered that aspect of the Church that guarantees the reality of the Church as Church. The bishops of the "Historic Church," as one occasionally hears it described, are held to be the organic connection between apostolic times and the present. The bishops are the guarantors of doctrinal and administrative unity and continuity. It was the bishops who were the vital link which passed on the teaching and practice of the Apostles, who in their various councils discriminated between true doctrine and heresy, and formulated the canonical tradition which regulates the everyday life of the Church to this day.

At the same time, the bishops—the episcopacy, taken as an institution—has become, in a way, strangely alienated from the life of most Orthodox Catholic Christians. In most churches, as Fr. Lawrence poignantly points out, the local bishop is symbolized by a chair which is reserved for him alone, but which for most of the time remains vacant. Indeed, most bishops are lucky to visit all their parishes within the time of any given year. There are places in the Orthodox world where one diocese may consist of hundreds of parishes, most of which may never see the diocesan bishop after the consecration of the Church.

In this compact and understandable book, Fr. Lawrence Farley has traced the history and development of the historic episcopacy from the beginnings of the Church to the present day. In addition, he offers reasons for what many see as the distance of the bishop's office from ordinary parish life. He also offers some suggestions to make the office both more visible and more accessible. Whether one agrees with his suggestions or not, they are important if for no other reason than to initiate a long-needed conversation on the subject.

+ Archbishop Melchizedek
of Pittsburgh and Western Pennsylvania
Orthodox Church in America

INTRODUCTION

THE EMPTY THRONE
The Episcopate in Today's Church

IN OUR LITTLE CHURCH IN LANGLEY, B.C., there is a chair on which no one sits, nor would anyone ever dare to. We have many chairs and places to sit—we have benches along the sides of the nave (but no pews), chairs in the narthex for overflow visitors, chairs in the church hall for our post-Liturgy lunch. We have chairs in the library. We have places to sit in the altar. But this chair remains empty, as if there were an invisible RESERVED sign resting upon it. It is found in the back of the altar area, and it is the episcopal throne, in its traditional place. (In churches using the Greek style of church architecture, the bishop's throne is located outside the altar, on the south side of the nave.) It is clearly episcopal, for it is a part of the *synthronon* or bench for the clergy to sit on during the reading of the lessons at Liturgy, and in our church it is the only part of the bench that comes with armrests.

Sometimes leaving the throne vacant feels a little like reserving a chair for Elijah at a Jewish *bris*: one always keeps the chair available, even if one never expects its occupant to actually show up. If the sacramental reality of Christ's true Body and Blood in the Eucharist has been called "the Real Presence," the bishop's reality in the Eucharist might be called "the Real Absence": we have his picture in the narthex; we elevate and pronounce his name repeatedly throughout all the services; we have his crucial signature on our *antimension*; we love him and have him always in our prayers and in our hearts. But despite all this, he is pretty much never actually here.

In this, our bishop is like every other bishop I have ever heard of. His own cathedral city and home (the so-called "see," from the Latin *sedes*, or "seat") is many miles away, and he is very busy taking care of his diocese and his many parishes. Not being able to bilocate, of course he can only be in one place at a time, and so most parishes have to do without the bishop's actual presence for most of the time.

When he does come to visit, it is an occasion of joy, and celebration, and high festivity. We bake special bread, which we offer him along with salt as the traditional gifts of welcome when he first enters. Everyone wants to see him and get his blessing, to exchange a few words with him. (I always make sure that our catechumens in particular get some time with him.) At the service, we pull out all the liturgical stops as we vest him and make things as fully glorious as we can. The choir has been practicing the special music well in advance of his arrival, as have the subdeacons. Lots of photographs are taken when he comes. Everyone is happy when he visits.

Note the verb in the last sentence: We are happy when he *visits*. It is this verb and this reality that most differentiates our situation from that of the early Church. In the days prior to Constantine, and even afterward in the days of St. John Chrysostom, the bishop never *visited* a church any more than I can be said to *visit* my little parish in Langley. I don't visit my church; I am there because I am the pastor. So it was in the days of Chrysostom: he didn't visit the Church of the Hagia Sophia; he was there all the time, because he was its pastor—that is, because he was its bishop.

And it was not just the church in the imperial capital that experienced its bishop as its normal Sunday morning pastor and weekly preacher. Every church was like that. The bishop was everywhere the pastor of the local church. And in that day, the local church was really local. Every little village, hamlet, town, or city had its own bishop, so that his "church" (what we now call his "diocese") consisted of the village or city where he lived, along with the surrounding countryside. (We even see this reflected in our Liturgy today, when we pray for Christians in "every city and country"—for by "country" is not meant "nation," but "countryside," the region surrounding the city.)

The bishop was the local pastor, the one who blessed and presided at every baptism, who anointed all in his church who were sick, who excommunicated the straying, and who reconciled the excommunicated back into the communion of the Church when they repented. He was assisted in his pastoral work and deliberations by a committee of presbyters and further helped by his deacons. But he was the face of the local church, the pastoral face upon which all the faithful looked every Sunday. In the early days, he was chosen by them and was bound to them until he died. He never "visited" his church, for he never went away.

A celebration of the Eucharist was unthinkable without the presidency of the bishop. We see this in a rule in an Egyptian Church Order that declares that a community of Christians cannot have their own bishop if they only number twelve persons. This of course tells us there were some little enclaves of Christians numbering less than twelve that still wanted their own bishop—otherwise the canon would have been unnecessary. This reveals as nothing else could the importance of the bishop to the local church in those early days. If the number of Christians grew in a village or city so that all could not meet in the same place, then the bishop would deputize one of the presbyters to serve the overflow group. But the bishop was still the main pastor of the village or city, the hub around which Christian life in that area revolved.

This means things have changed dramatically in the life of the local church. Now a presbyter, not the bishop, is the local pastor, for a bishop's church or diocese is now no longer a single community and its outlying countryside, but a sizable area consisting often of many cities and villages and vast distances. (Our own bishop has all of Canada for his diocese.) He can only visit each of his parishes once in a while and thus can maintain only a slight familiarity with the parishioners there. For day-to-day pastoral care, the parishioners rely not on the bishop, who often lives a great distance away and is busy with many other parishes, but on the local presbyter. He is their priest (a title which once normally described not the presbyter but the bishop). He is the one who gets the late-night emergency call to the hospital. He is the one who presides at the normal Sunday Eucharist, who baptizes the babies and catechumens, who anoints the sick, hears the confessions, and buries the dead. The bishop is loved and respected, but he functions as a beloved but distant uncle more than as a father. Things have changed.

Canonically and constitutionally, of course, things remain what they have always been. Gregory Dix, writing some time ago in his chapter "Ministry in the Early Church" in Kirk's large volume *The Apostolic Ministry*, distinguishes between what he calls the "constitutional" history of the episcopal office and the "administrative" one. Constitutionally, the office remains what it was from apostolic days: a ministry of shepherding, consecrating, ordaining, and (for the Anglican Dix in

Britain) confirming. But administratively the office underwent many changes. Dix recounts:

> There is the first stage [in Britain] when the bishop is above all an evangelist, a missionary monk. Under the Heptarchy he becomes something not very readily distinguishable from a tribal wizard. Under the Anglo-Saxon monarchy he becomes a royal counselor . . . passing by slow degrees into a great feudal landlord and then a national noble. After this, both before and after the Reformation, he is primarily the great civil servant. Later still he becomes the somewhat torpid grandee of the eighteenth century. Finally he is translated into the Victorian philanthropist and the modern spiritual bureaucrat.[1]

Obviously, Dix writes here only of bishops in his native Britain, but his point holds for bishops in all places, in that while the bishop's constitutional role remains constant, his administrative role is in flux. "Continuity of name does not necessarily imply continuity of function."[2] So it is that although the name of *bishop* has remained constant through Christian history and his constitutional role has remained unchanged, his administrative role has changed almost out of all recognition.

To truly help our bishops in their ongoing tasks, it is necessary to understand the history of the office and to see how it has changed administratively since pre-Nicene days. That is

---

1 Gregory Dix, "Ministry in the Early Church," in K. E. Kirk, *The Apostolic Ministry* (London: Hodder & Stoughton, 1946), pp. 187–188.
2 Ibid., p. 189.

not because the pre-Nicene period constituted a "golden age" of church history, but because it is only then that we first get to examine in some detail how the Church was structured in apostolic days and how it was meant to function. As we will see, though there is little in the New Testament which would help us learn how the church leadership actually interacted with the rest of the Church, many of these details can be found in the literature of the second and third centuries—details of an office first established by the apostles as part of the deposit of the Faith.

The present relationship of bishop to presbyter and parish in Orthodoxy is the fruit of a long and convoluted development, paralleling that of the bishop's office in Britain that Dix recounted. Therefore, we will attempt to summarize some of those changes in the chapters to come, to show how we arrived at our present situation. After a quick survey of the long evolution of the bishop's office in the Eastern part of the Church, we will offer some concluding reflections.

We begin at the beginning, in the apostolic first century.

THE BISHOP IN THE FIRST CENTURY
The Hidden President

Some suggest the first century is not the right place to begin to examine the episcopal office, on the basis that such an office did not then exist. In this reading of church history, the episcopal office (usually called "the monepiscopate," to differentiate the single bishop as head of his local community from a supposedly earlier situation where there was not a single leader) did not arise until the mid-second century, or perhaps in some places even later. In this understanding, Church writers such as Irenaeus (who died about AD 200) or Eusebius of Caesarea (who died about 340) were simply being anachronistic when they spoke of the existence of bishops in the first century, as they read back into an earlier time their own experience of church life. Thus when Irenaeus lists[3] the bishops of Rome in sequence from the apostles to his own day as Linus, Anacletus, Clement, Evaristus, Alexander, Sixtus, Telephorus, Hyginus, Pius, Anicetus, Soter, Eleutherius, he was misreading his history, since the earliest "bishops" on his list were not the monepiscopal kind of bishops he knew.

Granted that the episcopal office developed from the time of the apostles to the time of Irenaeus, is it true that the bishop's office did not exist in the first century, but that it was the creation of a later day? We begin examining the question by looking at the New Testament, for pretty much everything we know about the Church of the first century is contained there.

The New Testament Material

Some material relating to local church leadership can be found in Paul's Epistle to the Philippians. Paul writes from his prison in Rome, where he sits awaiting trial. One of his reasons for writing the Philippians was to thank them for sending him a gift of money, which arrived safely, brought by their messenger Epaphroditus. Epaphroditus, however, had suffered illness in the performance of this duty, and Paul therefore felt it necessary to send him back home lest he should die. He therefore sent him back bearing the letter to the Philippians, commending him for his service and heroic sacrifice and bidding the other Philippians to "receive him in the Lord with all joy and

---

3   *Against Heresies*, 3,3,3.

to honor such men, for he nearly died for the work of Christ, risking his life to complete your service to me" (Phil. 2:29–30). As well as wanting to spare Epaphroditus possible disgrace for running out on Paul (as his detractors may have thought), Paul also wanted the Philippians to know that he indeed "received in full payment . . . the gifts you sent, a fragrant offering, a sacrifice acceptable and pleasing to God" (Phil. 4:18).

It is perhaps for this reason that Paul begins his epistle to the Philippians in this way: "Paul and Timothy, slaves of Christ Jesus, to all the saints in Christ Jesus who are at Philippi, with the bishops (Gr. *episkopois*) and deacons (Gr. *diakonois*)" (Phil. 1:1). The bishops and deacons were those in the local Philippian community responsible for collecting and sending the gifts, and for this reason Paul singles them out in his initial address.

As is well known, the term *diakonos* simply means "servant," one who fulfills the will of another, and is the word used by Paul to describe himself in his apostolic ministry (e.g., 1 Cor. 3:5) and even to describe Christ (Rom. 15:8). In its secular usage, it refers to one who was responsible for certain welfare duties within the city, or an attendant in a temple. The word *episkopos* has a long history. It described tutors, inspectors, scouts, army officers, watchmen, and superintendents. The Essene communities were administered by an officer termed a *mebaqqer* (corresponding to the Greek *episkopos*), who was viewed as their spiritual leader and who administered the finances.[4] We may understand the bishops addressed by Paul as men exercising oversight in the church community there.

Episkopos is not the only term Paul uses when speaking of leadership in the Church, and it seems that terms denoting pastoral office or pastoral function were then quite fluid. In Paul's First Epistle to the Corinthians (12:28), he speaks of the gifts not only of prophecy, but also of a ministry of "helps" and of "administration." Could these be references to the functions later encompassed by the terms *deacons* and *bishops/presbyters*? Paul also refers to gifts of *diakonia* and *didaskalia*, "serving" and "teaching," in Romans 12:7, as well as to "shepherds and teachers" in Ephesians 4:11. It is possible he is referring to ministries of serving and overseeing, using a number of terms to describe the function at a time when the terminology for them was still evolving. Certainly it is difficult to find much difference in meaning between the functions of an overseer (or bishop), an administrator, and a shepherd. We conclude that Paul's earliest letters reveal a single office of pastoral oversight, sometimes referred to as the office of the bishop.

In examining the Church's leadership ministry in the first century, we turn also to the Acts of the Apostles. There we meet the term "presbyter" or "elder" (Gr. *presbyteros*) as an established feature of church life. Thus relief funds were sent to

---

4 Gerald Hawthorne, Word Biblical Commentary, volume 43, *Philippians* (Vancouver, B.C.: Word Publishing, 1983), p. 8.

the poor of Jerusalem "by the hand of Barnabas and Saul to the presbyters" (Acts 11:30). Thus Paul and Barnabas "appointed presbyters for them in every church" on the way back to Syria (Acts 14:23). Thus, in Jerusalem, the council that gathered to discuss the divisive controversy of whether or not to circumcise Gentile converts was a gathering of "the apostles and presbyters," and its decisions were conveyed to the wider church in a letter from "the apostles and the brothers who are presbyters" (Acts 15:2, 23). Clearly, Luke expects his readers to have some familiarity with the institution, especially since he does not narrate the institution of the presbytery.

Given the Jewish background to the presbytery, there is no reason why the apostles would not have reproduced a version of this universal Jewish institution in their own Christian synagogues.[5] Every Jewish community in Palestine and in the Diaspora was ruled by a body of presbyters (in Hebrew, *zeqenim*), men who were elected for life. In the larger Jewish communities, there was also an annually elected executive committee chosen from among this body, consisting of a chairman, a treasurer, and others. Unlike men exercising public office in the secular Gentile world, these Jews were admitted to their office through the laying on of hands, by analogy with Moses laying his hands upon Joshua, and they were considered as set apart by God for their spiritual tasks.[6]

---

5   Compare James 2:2: "If a man comes into your synagogue"
6   Dix, op. cit., p. 233.

Among their tasks were helping the poor, the upkeep of local schools, and (significantly) the determination of who did or did not belong to the local Jewish community. A Jew could be brought before them for trial and discipline and could be cast out of the synagogue (compare Matt. 10:17; John 9:22). The parallels to the Christian office of presbyter are striking and add credibility to the suggestion that the presbyters Luke speaks of in his Acts narrative were modeled upon the Jewish presbyters encountered in all the synagogues of Palestine and the Diaspora.

In Acts 20:17–35, Luke narrates a speech given by Paul to the "presbyters of the church" from Ephesus (Acts 20:17). In that speech, Paul calls them shepherds, telling them to "take heed to yourselves and to all the flock in which the Holy Spirit has placed you as bishops to shepherd the church of God" (20:28). Here we see the identity of the roles of presbyter and bishop (and even shepherd), for the words *presbyteros* and *episkopos* are used here interchangeably.

We thus have a number of terms used to designate the local leaders of the Christian communities of the first century who exercised a ministry of administration: they are called shepherds, presbyters, and bishops. That all these terms refer to the same office is further indicated by passages occurring both in Luke's narrative and also in the pastoral epistles, to which we now turn. (Whether the pastoral epistles are authentically Pauline does not critically affect the issue, since whether or not they were the work of Paul, they reflect first-century terminological usage.)

In the First Epistle to Timothy, the author writes of two offices only, those of bishop and deacon (1 Tim. 3:1–13). Yet elsewhere in the epistle the author speaks in passing of presbyters (1 Tim. 4:14; 5:17–19[7]). This strongly suggests that the bishop of 3:1f and the presbyter of 5:17 are the same. We see the same identification of bishop and presbyter in the Epistle to Titus also. Here Paul instructs Titus to "appoint presbyters in every city" (1:5) and then goes on to give the necessary qualifications—namely, that "the bishop must be above reproach," and so forth (1:7). Clearly here the two terms designate the same office, just as they do in the speech Luke narrated in Acts 20.

Thus the biblical material offers the following picture: By analogy with normal Jewish synagogue organization, the apostles established in every city presbyters/bishops, men charged with the task of being shepherds for their local communities. These existed in a plurality in each community, even as they did in Judaism. The original fluidity of terminology observed in Paul's earliest epistles soon gave way to the settled use of the terms *bishop* and *presbyter* to describe the leaders exercising oversight. They were assisted in the local government of

---

7 And, though with less probability, 5:1. Analogy with older women in 5:2 leads one to suppose this is a reference to an "older man" (thus rendered in NASB, RSV, TEV, Phillips, etc.), and not to the office of *presbyteros*.

their churches by deacons, so that these two were the main office-bearers in each local Christian community.

Material from the Late First Century

In the later part of the first century, we also find two other documents that help us in examining what the pastoral office looked like at that time: the Didache and the First Epistle of Clement.

The Didache is a composite document, dealing with a number of topics. Because of the simplicity and Jewish quality of its prayers, the continued existence of roving prophets claiming support from the local communities, and the mention (relevant to our own study) of the need of the local church to appoint for themselves bishops and deacons, it is often dated to the end of the first century. Its author knows only of the offices of bishop and deacon. In chapter 15:1–2 we read, "Appoint for yourselves bishops and deacons worthy of the Lord, men who are humble and not avaricious and true and approved, for they too carry out the ministry of the prophets and teachers. You must not, therefore, despise them, for they are your honored men, along with the prophets and teachers." (We note in passing that the office of teacher is still distinguished from that of bishop/presbyter, just as in Eph. 4:11, where teachers and shepherds are mentioned together but are not identical. In 1 Tim. 5:17, the presbyter may labor at teaching, but this is not required. If he does, he is therefore "worthy of double honor." This is further evidence of an early date.)

The Didache therefore witnesses to a situation where the two main church offices at the end of the first century were bishops and deacons. This is also the situation we find in the Epistle of Clement. The author of the epistle writes in the name of the church at Rome to the church at Corinth, rebuking them for deposing presbyters there without due cause. The epistle is traditionally dated to the last decade of the first century, during the persecution of Domitian (81–96) or the beginning of Nerva's reign (96–98), which well accords with the internal references to "the sudden and repeated misfortunes and reverses that have happened to us" (1:1). In reminding the Corinthians of the venerable and apostolic dignity of the office of bishop, the author writes:

> Preaching in the country and in the towns, [the apostles] appointed their first fruits when they had tested them by the Spirit, to be bishops and deacons for the future believers. And this was no new thing they did, for indeed something had been written about bishops and deacons many years ago; for somewhere thus the Scripture says, "I will appoint their bishops in righteousness and their deacons in faith" [Is. 60:17 LXX]. . . . Our apostles knew through our Lord Jesus Christ that there would be strife over the name of the bishop [i.e., over the bishop's office]. For this reason therefore having received complete foreknowledge, they appointed the leaders mentioned earlier and afterwards they gave the offices a permanent character; that is, if they should die, other approved men should succeed to their ministry. . . . For it will be no

small sin for us if we depose from the bishop's office those who have offered the gifts blamelessly and in holiness. Blessed are those presbyters who have gone on ahead, who took their departure at a mature and fruitful age, for they need no longer fear that someone may remove them from their established place. (42:4–5; 44:1–2, 4–5)

Here we note the author speaks of "strife over the name of bishop" and then goes on to speak of "presbyters who have gone on ahead" and therefore were spared this strife. Thus in the last decade of the first century, the two terms *bishop* and *presbyter* are still used as interchangeably as they are in Acts 20:17f and Titus 1:5f. The roles of bishop/presbyter and deacon still represent the only two ministries of the church of an official and institutional nature.

The Establishment of the Monepiscopate: A Bloodless Coup?

We have seen that the material available from the first century overwhelmingly favors a view that the local leadership then consisted of deacons and bishops/presbyters. Yet by the very beginning of the next century, Ignatius of Antioch will be writing to the communities of Asia Minor and Rome, exhorting them to submit to their bishops and the presbyters with him, clearly indicating that the bishop has a different office from his presbyters. Given that Ignatius, dying in about AD 107, must have been bishop for a few years before his arrest and martyrdom, this means he flourished in the latter part of the first century. He is emphatic that the office of the bishop is a separate one from that of the presbyter. Moreover, he clearly thought not only that the churches to which he was writing had such bishops, but that these bishops held a different office from the presbyters who were with them. He did not write as someone advancing a new idea, but as one confident that all the other churches in the world shared the structure he knew.

Thus he wrote that bishops were "appointed throughout the world" (To the Eph. 3.2); without the triad of deacons, bishop, and presbyters, "no group can be called a church" (To the Trall. 3.1); those who "call a man bishop but do everything without regard for him do not appear to act in good conscience, since they do not validly meet together" (To the Magn. 4); all must "follow the bishop as Jesus Christ followed the Father" (To the Smyr. 8.1).

The first-century material we have seen spoke only of bishops and deacons, but Ignatius, who lived at that time, wrote as if all the churches of the world had bishops, presbyters, and deacons. What then are we to make of this? If all the churches in the first century used the terms *bishop* and *presbyter* interchangeably, how can we account for Ignatius writing to them as if the two offices were different?

Some suggest that the monepiscopal arrangement promoted by Ignatius represented a radical departure from past polity, a reordering of the apostolic arrangement. In that apostolic arrangement, there were only coequal presbyters, with no one presbyter claiming any kind of preeminence over his fellows, and then this polity was replaced by one in which one of the presbyters indeed claimed and took preeminence over the others. Some suggest the revolution occurred at different times in different places, with Antioch becoming monepiscopal first, and Rome holding out somewhat longer, but eventually, the new and revolutionary arrangement prevailed, so that by the middle half of the second century or so, every church had a monepiscopal government.

There are problems with this supposition. We know from the tenor of writings in the subapostolic period that the Church was very conservative in its approach, so that the term *apostolic* meant something sacred and inviolable. Are we really to suppose that a radical alteration of something so fundamental as the local church leadership established by the apostles would have provoked no protest anywhere?[8] And there is the added geographical problem. The "Vincentian canon" famously looks upon universality as a sure indicator of apostolic origin, and the monepiscopate certainly passes this test of universality. If a radical reordering of the structure of church leadership did occur, one would expect more global variety, with some groups

---

8 Some suggest that the apostle John was provoked by it, and denounced Ignatius under the name Diotrephes in 3 John 9 for ambitiously "putting himself first." But if John was denouncing the radical new arrangement, it is odd to find him a few verses later commending Demetrius for the same job (v. 12).

becoming monepiscopal, some more staunchly presbyterian, some congregational. But as it is, the churches throughout the entire world were all monepiscopal around the same time. There are virtually no exceptions, and absolutely no protest anywhere.

This deafening silence needs to be accounted for by any who assert that the monepiscopate was new in the second century. How could such a bloodless coup have taken place in communities so attached to all things apostolic—and while claiming apostolicity for the new arrangement, at that? For Ignatius writes not like a man agitating for a new and better system, but like a man (and a dying man at that) falling back in tenacious reliance upon old custom. So, where did the monepiscopal bishop come from?

One suggestion is that the bishop was simply the wandering prophet of the first century settling and putting down local roots. The Didache (ch. 13) says the prophet has the right to "settle" in any of the churches he visits. Perhaps the "new" monepiscopal bishop was simply the older prophet who ceased his wandering and settled down to take up his permanent residence in the Church? A prophet always enjoyed the right as an inspired man to give thanks at the meals however he liked (compare Didache, ch. 10). Perhaps this was the source of the later bishop's liturgical authority?

Despite providing a possible link between the first-century situation and that of the second century, it seems unlikely that the origin of the monarchical bishop can be found in the prophet of the first century. In the New Testament and later literature, the prophets are consistently viewed as having no personal authority apart from their inspired utterance. That is, it is their word that possesses authority, not themselves, and while their prophetic mantle would have resulted in great personal prestige, it never translated into personal authority to rule. Indeed, even in the New Testament their prophetic utterances were subjected to the local leaders (see 1 Cor. 14:29–30: "Let two or three prophets speak, and let the others pass judgment. But if a revelation is made to another who is seated [i.e., judging the prophecy], let the first [i.e., the prophet] keep silence").

Given this early subordination of the prophets to the leaders, it is inconceivable that a prophet could "settle" and assume authority over those leaders. Also, it is unlikely that the wandering prophets who created such problems for the author of the Didache (see warnings in ch. 11) would have existed in such universal profusion as to settle and take over in every church in the world. We are still left then to account for the smooth and silent transition from presbyters to bishop-and-presbyters by the early second century.

A Hidden President

I suggest the answer to the puzzle is to be sought in a hidden president, so that what we see in the Ignatian letters is not a radical change in the structure of ecclesial authority, but simply a shift in terminology as dictated by the new circumstances, "the sudden and repeated misfortunes and reverses" referred to by the epistle of Clement. The communities always had a single figure within them who presided, referred to a generation later as (not surprisingly) "the president."[9] As we will see below, the Christians in each city strove to meet together for their Eucharist all "in the same place," however many separate meetings they held elsewhere for prayer and study. The single Eucharist necessitated and required a single president to offer the eucharistic anaphora. All the presbyters might gather together for the Eucharist, but by definition only one could preside; only one mouth could utter the central prayer. In the early part of the first century, this presider had no special designation and did not need one. In Jerusalem (the church we know the most about from the New Testament), this presider was James (compare Acts 12:17; 15:13; 21:18). In Rome it was Clement. But though the president had no special designation beyond his name, each community had one presbyter who presided at the Eucharist.

Metropolitan John Zizioulas confirms this. In his work *Eucharist, Bishop, Church*, he says, "This triad [bishop-presbyters-deacons] was the first linguistic form under which the Bishop appeared in history as a specific and complete rank, initially known only by the personal name of the officeholder and implicit within the collective term 'the presbyters' . . . it

---

9 Thus Justin Martyr, in his *Apology*, ch. 65.

follows that the office of Bishop exists even in the apostolic period."[10] When an apostle visited the local community, obviously the apostle would preside. In the apostle's absence, the eldest presbyter/bishop would preside, and it was natural to regard him as, in a special way, the successor to the apostles, for liturgically, that is exactly how he functioned.

Why the change of terminology, reserving the term *bishop* to one of the presbyters who presided at the Eucharist? I would suggest the external fact of persecution and the internal threat of heresy made unity all the more necessary. In such times of stress, people tend to quarrel and scatter (compare St. Paul's exhortation to unity when persecution began to fall upon him, in Phil. 1:27–30), and thus reinforced unity became an urgent need. That unity, as we shall see below, found its source and expression in the single Eucharist, and so the president at the Eucharist necessarily came to the fore. Thus the term *overseer/bishop* was reserved to the one who oversaw and presided at the Eucharist at which all gathered.

There was therefore no protest because there was no substantial change beyond a simple change of terminology. The presbyters ruled jointly in the first century, but (as we shall see) they continued to rule in the second century also, for the bishop's task was primarily liturgical. The local churches did not submit only to the bishop, but to the bishop *and the presbyters*, as to a

---

10 Zizioulas, *Eucharist, Bishop, Church*, Brookline: Holy Cross Press, 2001, p. 64.

single authority. Thus we read in Ignatius's letter that the presbyters were but "strings attuned to an [episcopal] lyre" (To the Eph. 4.1). The faithful were to "be united with the bishop *and with those who lead*"; they were not to do anything "without the bishop *and the presbyters*" (To the Magn. 6.2, 7.1); they were to "do nothing without the bishop, [and] *be subject also to the council of presbyters*" (To the Trall. 2.2).

The monepiscopate did nothing to impair presbyteral authority. It simply brought the head presbyter and main liturgist to the fore in a time of crisis when the need of the day was for greater unity in the face of increasing onslaught. The bishop's role as the head and liturgizing presbyter also existed in the first century, since someone had to offer corporate prayer at the time when they all gathered *epi to auto*, in the same place. By the early and mid-second century, the terminological shift had been completed, and all churches were recognizably monepiscopal, both in structure and in terminology.

Overview of the Episcopate in the First Century

We have seen that in the first century, the apostles appointed a plurality of leaders within the local Christian communities. Since the apostles came from a Jewish environment, they naturally reproduced the Jewish forms of leadership with which they were familiar and appointed presbyters for leaders, putting them into office through the laying on of hands, just as Jewish presbyters were appointed. Descriptive terms abounded at first, and these men were called *presbyters, bishops, leaders, shepherds, administrators* (e.g., Acts 11:30; Phil. 1:1; Heb. 13:17; Eph. 4:11; 1 Cor. 12:28). Eventually two terms were settled upon, and the governing leaders were referred to as both *bishops* and *presbyters*.

Even so, since the Christians in any given community met weekly at the same location for a single Eucharist, one of the presbyters/bishops had a greater prominence and a more important role—that of presiding each week at the Eucharist. A terminological refinement seems to have begun first in Asia Minor, and the president came to be known not just as a presbyter or a bishop, but as *the* bishop. As the Church grew and entered a more intense and prolonged time of persecution in the second century, the bishop's importance continued to grow and to be reflected in the liturgical tradition.

Furthermore, beginning in the second century we can find more literary evidence for how the bishop and presbyters functioned and interacted and what their roles were. It is to this evidence that we now turn.

CHAPTER TWO

THE BISHOP IN THE PRE-NICENE CHURCH
The Voice at the Altar

A Single Assembly

IN THE NEW TESTAMENT we find only one church per city: the church in Corinth, or the church in Thessalonica (1 Cor. 1:2; 1 Thess. 1:1), but the churches (plural) in the region of Galatia (Gal. 1:2). This usage is consistent throughout the New Testament in passages that contain mention of place. Paul may speak of "the church" in the abstract, without any mention of its locale (e.g., in Eph. 3:10, where he writes that "through the church the manifold wisdom of God is now made known to the principalities and powers in the heavenlies"), but when he specifies a locale for the church, he always refers to the church in the singular. Thus we find "the church of God" in Corinth, not "the churches of God" there. The use of the single noun points to the fact that all Christians in the city gathered together as a single assembly.

Furthermore, the term "church" meant not just any assembly of the local Christians, but the eucharistic assembly. When Paul speaks to the Corinthians in 1 Corinthians 11:18 of "assembling as a church," he refers to their eucharistic assembly, so that to despise that Eucharist by their actions is to "despise the church of God" (v. 22). The Eucharist is what makes a gathering a church. Also, of all the persons Paul greets in Romans 16, only Prisca and Aquila are greeted along with "the church in their house" (Rom. 16:3–5), for they alone hosted the single Eucharist of all the Christians in Rome. It is the same with Gaius, whose greetings Paul conveyed from Corinth, who was host to Paul "and to the whole church"—that is, the whole church in Corinth. There were many Christians in these cities, and perhaps many places for meetings throughout the week, but only one place where all assembled as a church for the eucharistic assembly. The bishop in this time therefore presided over the eucharistic assembly of all the Christians in his city.

Sometimes, it seems, this norm and ideal were not possible, if the large numbers and limited space of housing prevented such a gathering of all "in one place." One imagines the multitudes of Christians converted in Jerusalem could not all fit into one dwelling, so that their eucharistic "breaking bread [*kat' oikon*]" (Acts 2:46) must have involved them sharing their meals "from house to house" (thus the NASB translation) and not all in a single house. Luke narrates the conversion of three thousand on the Day of Pentecost alone; a little later the number of converts has increased to "five thousand" (Acts 4:4). James tells Paul upon his arrival in Jerusalem that there are in the city "ten thousands" of Christians (Acts 21:20). Even allowing for hyperbole (especially in the last instance), there are simply too many to fit into a single dwelling. The norm may have been assembly within a single dwelling, but it seems that in Jerusalem, at least, the ideal gave way to practicality.

This is hinted at in the epistles of Ignatius as well. Ignatius is emphatic that the local Christians must gather about their bishop and their presbyters, finding in this assembly alone their authentic unity. Yet even he allows for the fact that sometimes another overflow gathering must occur. In his epistle to the Smyrnaeans, he writes, "Let no one do anything that has to do with the church apart from the bishop. Let that be held a valid Eucharist which is under the bishop *or one to whom he shall have committed it*" (Smyrnaeans, ch. 8.1). The unity of the church was realized and expressed liturgically by the single Eucharist at which the bishop presided.

But ultimately, it was the bishop's blessing and the local Christians' relationship with the bishop that mattered, not his physical presence. His physical presence was normative, but not indispensable, so that his presidency at the Eucharist might be validly delegated to a fellow presbyter. But this does not detract from the norm or the ideal. As Ignatius said, "Wherever the bishop appears, there let the congregation be" (Smyrn. 8.2), and this vision prevailed. Even in Jerusalem a few centuries later, the local congregation would join the bishop for liturgy, wherever he was. If he served in a smaller chapel on a feast day, then all went there with him, and the larger basilica stood empty.

The Unity of the Local Church as a Wall of Safety

As said above, the renewed emphasis on the unity of the church that prompted reserving the title of bishop for the presiding presbyter had its origin in the dangers of the times. It is not simply that persecution was renewed after the time of the emperor Domitian (a persecution that lay behind the determined spirit of the Book of Revelation). And it was not just that heresies came to the fore, making the bishop's teaching all the more important as the norm for determining which assemblies represented the true Church of God. We will misjudge the temper of the times and fail to understand the need for unity unless we appreciate how the Christians then viewed the world. In a word, they viewed it as fatally polluting and dangerous, and it was only in the unity of the Church that a soul found safety.

The thought is not new to the second century. As early as the Acts of the Apostles, Christians perceived that conversion to Christ meant "turning from darkness to light and from the dominion of Satan to God" (Acts 26:18). They knew from St. Paul that to be expelled from the Church meant being delivered to Satan for the destruction of one's flesh (1 Cor. 5:5), and that Satan was "the god of this age" (2 Cor. 4:4). They knew from St. John that "the whole world lies in the power of the Evil One" (1 John 5:19). Joining the Church meant crossing into an entirely different moral universe, with the inevitable resultant alienation of the new convert from his surrounding culture. Conversion to Christ and membership in the Church involved a total break with one's past. In the Church's liturgical tradition, exorcisms were required to qualify candidates for baptism; the chasm between Church and world was too great to cross without this added level of purification. So contaminating was the world that even a pagan who had become a catechumen was regarded as unfit to join with the baptized Christians as they prayed for the world or to exchange the kiss of peace at their Eucharist.

It was the walls of the Church (that is, her discipline) that kept the pollution safely at bay and allowed the Christians to be in the world, but not of it. Converts would enter through the gate, pass from the world into the Church, and find safety within her walls. The sacramental gate through which they passed, of course, was baptism. That meant those guarding the gates had a tremendously important and even saving function. The ones guarding the gates were the presbyters, who exercised judgment concerning church membership, and the bishop, who liturgized and presided at baptism itself.

The importance of the Church's walls accounts for the

seriousness with which Ignatius's readers took his exhortations to unity and the horror that all the early Church held for schism, for all thought schism was damnable. Indeed, even those who, like Pope Stephen of Rome, thought the schismatic churches had true sacraments admitted that those sacraments were unavailing as long as those receiving them remained in schism. The fatal consequences of schism made the Church's unity all the more important. And this saving unity was liturgically expressed by the single eucharistic assembly gathered around the bishop.

The Independence of Cities and Churches in the First Centuries

The metaphorical walls of the Church found an unconscious echo in the actual walls surrounding the city in which the church found itself and by which it defined itself (for example, as "the church in Corinth"). Cities in the first centuries of the common era maintained a fierce independence, and their citizens took pride in them to a degree scarcely imaginable today. In North America today, citizens regard themselves primarily as belonging to a country ("my country, right or wrong," not "my city, right or wrong"), and whatever pride they may feel in belonging to a city is eclipsed by their national pride. Being an American, for example, is more important than being an inhabitant of Des Moines. Americans pledge their allegiance to the national flag, not to symbols of their city.

These national realities did not exist in the same way in the ancient Roman world. One was conscious of being (for example) a Cappadocian or a Galatian, and of belonging to a particular region, sharing geographical landmarks and speaking perhaps a particular dialect. But pride in one's city was more emotionally important than these regional loyalties, so that when St. Paul boasted he was "a citizen of no mean city" (Acts 21:39), it was Tarsus that swelled his heart, not Cilicia.

In the first centuries, obviously, these cities dwelt under the shadow of Rome, enjoying the *pax Romana* and paying whatever taxes and dues were required. But the cities then enjoyed a marked degree of independence. This independence would decrease throughout the next two centuries, as the central imperial government clamped down more and more, but in the first century civic independence was still strong. The Roman world consisted of a large federation of self-administering city-republics held together by the framework of the Empire.[11] An Antiochene man thought of himself primarily as a citizen of Antioch, and it was within this independent city-republic that he sought his honor—including whatever honor could accrue from the larger Roman world, not from his connections with (for example) the wider Syria.

This is important in looking at the independence of churches in those centuries, for then the churches were independent in a

---

11 Dix, "Ministry in the Early Church," in *The Apostolic Ministry*, ed. K. Kirk (London: Hodder & Stoughton, 1946), p. 274.

way scarcely imaginable today. We Orthodox think of ourselves primarily as belonging to Orthodoxy, or perhaps to our particular Orthodox jurisdiction. What matters is that one is in the OCA or the Greek jurisdiction, and which parish one attends is largely irrelevant. The canon of Scripture read in Vancouver is identical to that read in New York, as are the prescribed text of the Liturgy, the fasting rules, and the Creed.

This is almost the opposite of the customs in the pre-Nicene Church. Though of course the consciousness of belonging to a worldwide Church was strong, the day-to-day details of ecclesiastical existence were determined by membership in the local church. Each local church had its own canon of Scripture, its own creed, its own anaphora, its own patterns of fasting and canonical discipline. Obviously the differences between the practices of the churches were not very great (one church may or may not have read the Book of James liturgically, for example), but such differences abounded.

The mature took it in stride, and Ambrose is famously reported to have said to a perplexed parishioner that these things were matters of comparative indifference: when in Rome, he fasted according to the Roman custom, despite it being a different praxis from his own Milanese one.[12] These differences were possible and ruffled no one's feathers—not only because they did not concern the basics of the Faith, but also

---

12 Thus he famously said, "When I am at Rome, I fast on a Saturday; when I am at Milan, I do not. Follow the custom of the church where you are."

because of the strong tradition of local church independence.

The bishop also reflected this strong tradition of local independence. He was defined by his relationship with his flock, and they were defined by their relationship with him. The unity of a bishop with his local church was strong—so much so that if a bishop fell into heresy or schism and the local laity stood by their man, there was little the wider Church could do about it. The wider Church exercised over the local churches authority of influence, not of command, for there was simply no machinery of enforcement in the pre-Nicene Church.

The bishops of the larger churches, such as Alexandria or Antioch, doubtless felt that their responsibility to the truth in certain controversies meant they should promote their views to the smaller churches who looked to them for guidance, and these local primates spoke with the clear expectation that the smaller churches would follow their lead. Accordingly, they advised and sometimes intervened to correct problems in the churches that looked to them for leadership (such as Rome's intervention in the affairs of Corinth, reflected in the letter of 1 Clement). But there was no recognized way to compel other churches to accept their authority if they insisted on defiance. The authority of the larger and more important churches was a moral one, one based on custom and on whatever prestige they could muster.

This kind of advice and intervention was also comparatively rare, and one can see why. Bishops might pronounce, and local councils might make pronouncements, but in the absence of machinery to enforce compliance, the final say lay with the decisions of the local church. And sometimes the wider Church did not appreciate what a local church actually decided. For example, a council of bishops might depose one of their number for heresy or other misdemeanor, but if the erring bishop's local church stood by him, there was little the rest of the Church could do to replace the erring bishop. Later on, the emperor could drive away the erring bishop and install his "canonical" replacement by force of arms, but even then he could not compel the local church to attend the replacement's Liturgy. These early councils were, in fact, merely consultative gatherings rather than bodies capable of overriding local decisions.

The bishop at this time was primarily the bishop of his city, identified with his flock and considered to be married to his church—to such a degree that a transfer to another see was compared to adultery. For this reason it was inconceivable for a bishop to be transferred to another city/see for reasons of career advancement. This became enshrined in the canons, such as Nicea canon 15, which pronounces the attempted move null and returns the bishop to his original see. The practice of transfer became more and more common as time progressed and as the episcopate began to be seen more and more as an attractive career option. But the abuse never replaced the original vision, which linked the bishop permanently to his local church.

We see this same localization of leadership with the pre-Nicene presbyters as well. A presbyter was likewise ordained for a specific community, and his authority was tied to it. He was not a presbyter at large. Thus Cyprian of Carthage announced to his flock that the presbyter Numidicus, formerly a presbyter of another church, is to join the presbyters of Carthage as one of them. But by so doing, Numidicus has ceased to be a presbyter of his old church; it was not considered that his ordination or authority was transferrable. Numidicus, after his acceptance by Cyprian and his men, was not just a presbyter *in* Carthage, but also *of* Carthage.[13] In the early centuries, the walls of the local church were strong indeed.

The Authority of the Bishop

The authority of the bishop was not a delegated one, as if the people decided what they wanted at a general meeting and the bishop simply carried it out. He had his own divine authority, given through the apostles. It is important, however, to see exactly how that authority was given to him and in what it consisted.

The authority was given to the candidate for the episcopate by God, because it was God who chose the candidate for that office. This is clear from the ordination prayer for a bishop given in the *Apostolic Tradition* of Hippolytus. This prayer reads in part, "You who know the hearts of all, bestow upon this Your

---

13 Dix, op. cit., p. 280.

servant *whom You have chosen for the episcopate*, to feed Your flock."[14] Note that God is the One who chose the candidate to be bishop. But this divine choice is apparent only because the candidate is the clear choice of the people. In an earlier chapter we read of the selection process for the candidate:

> Let him be ordained bishop *who has been chosen by all the people*, and when he has been named and accepted by all, let the people assemble together with the presbytery and those bishops who are present, on the Lord's day. When all give consent, they shall lay hands on him, and the presbytery shall stand by and be still. And all shall keep silence, praying in their hearts for the descent of the Spirit, after which one of the bishops present, being asked by all, shall lay his hand on him who is being ordained bishop and pray.[15]

We note the continued reference in this rubric to "all": the candidate has been *chosen by all the people* and *accepted by all*. The people assemble along with the presbyters, so that the entirety of the local church is involved. *All* must give consent for the ordination, and *all* keep silence, praying in their hearts. The presiding bishop only prays after being *asked by all*. It is hard to imagine a greater degree of local participation in the ordination of a bishop, and it is easy to see how later tradition could so strongly identify the bishop with his flock. The consensus of the Spirit-bearing local church is taken as a sign that the ordination

---
14 *Apostolic Tradition*, ch. 3.
15 Op. cit., ch. 2.

is God's will as well as the people's will, and that God has spoken through the choice of His people.

The voice of the people, their Spirit-led cry of *axios*, was considered to be as important as the ordination ritual itself. Their *axios* or assent that the candidate was worthy came *before* the ordination and functioned as the authorization for the ordaining clergy to proceed—very different from current practice, where the people's *axios* is solicited *after* the ordination has taken place, so that it functions as a kind of ecclesiastical *mazel tov*. The ancient practice paralleled the eucharistic preface, where the celebrant said to the congregation, "Let us give thanks to the Lord," and they responded, "It is meet and right," authorizing the celebrant to continue to offer the anaphora.

The sacramental invocation of the Holy Spirit, whether upon the eucharistic Gifts or upon the episcopal candidate, involved prayer of the whole assembled church. Their liturgical assent was crucial to the bishop's authority and was as much a condition for his ordination as the ordination prayer itself. The other bishops (and the silently praying presbyters, according to the Hippolytean *Apostolic Tradition*) were indeed the ones who ordained the candidate a bishop by their prayer, for this prayer effectively called down the Holy Spirit. (The phrase in the ordination prayer reads, "Pour forth that power which is from You, of the princely Spirit which You granted through Your beloved Son Jesus Christ to Your holy apostles.") But God heard and answered their prayer of ordination because He

Himself had chosen the candidate for this office, revealing His choice through the consensus of the people. Thus the bishop's authority was rooted both in his free election by the people who knew him and wanted him for their bishop, and in the effectual prayer of the consecrating bishops asking God to pour forth His Spirit.

This, then, was the basis for the bishop's authority. But in what did this authority consist? In the pre-Nicene Church, it consisted of two things: authority to teach the truth, and authority to liturgize.

First of all, the bishop received authority and power from God to know and speak the truth. His first function was to teach, and his teaching formed the touchstone of orthodoxy. Indeed, the people would remain in communion with him only because he preached the truth, and intercommunion among bishops was predicated upon their mutual recognition of the same Gospel truth.

Upon ordination, the bishop received a *charisma* of truth, a spiritual gift through sacramental ordination. Irenaeus writes, "It is incumbent to obey the presbyters who are in the church—those who possess the succession from the apostles, those who, together with the succession of the episcopate, have received the certain gift of truth, according to the good pleasure of the Father."[16] This sets them apart from the heretics, who, not having continuity of teaching stretching back to the apostles, are

---

16 *Against Heresies*, 4, 26, 2.

also bereft of the spiritual gifts that are available only in the true Church. Historical continuity and sacramental power unite to qualify the bishops as the reliable teachers of truth.

Secondly, the bishop received authority to liturgize, to function as the Spirit-bearing church's mouth and voice, so that the church effectually invoked the Spirit through his prayers. All the faithful would pray in church, of course, with the presbyters standing with the bishop as his colleagues and college. But it was the bishop's voice they heard at the altar; it was the bishop who was authorized through ordination to preside at the sacramental services.

The ordination prayer mentioned in Hippolytus's *Apostolic Tradition* is very clear about this. It prays that the candidate may shepherd the holy flock and serve as God's high priest. This involved:

1. "ceaselessly propitiating God's countenance, offering Him the gifts of His holy church" (that is, offering the eucharistic sacrifice of the Liturgy);
2. "having authority to forgive sins" (that is, reconciling penitents, restoring them to the communion of the church);
3. "conferring orders according to God's bidding" (that is, ordaining);
4. "loosing every bond" (that is, a ministry of exorcism and healing).

All of these were liturgical functions. The bishop's main task was to preside at these services, standing at the head of the other presbyters and saying the prayers on behalf of all. God would hear the church's prayers offered by him because God had chosen him for this task and empowered him by His Spirit to perform it. The bishop, by virtue of his central liturgical role, was the center around which the life of the church revolved. His prayers "propitiated God's countenance" in the Liturgy; his prayers created other ministries in the local church, reconciled penitents to the church, and brought healing and deliverance.

He functioned as the pastoral face for the community. It was the people's relationship with him that defined and provided for their place in the worldwide Church. He was present and presided at every baptism. It was from his hand that the people received the Eucharist. It was his prayers that brought healing to them when they were sick; it was he that prayed for them after they reposed. In those days, a bishop never retired, and there were no assistant bishops. While the bishop lived, he served as pastor to his flock. They were accountable to him, and he was directly involved with them, either for praise or censure. The relationship between shepherd and flock was intensely close, and like the Good Shepherd, the bishop knew his flock by name (John 10:3).

The Authority of the Presbyters

We note first that presbyters were also chosen by the people. A presbyter was ordained to take his part in a college of presbyters, and apart from this college the presbyter had no authority.

The role and authority of the presbyters may be discerned from the prayer used to ordain them. In the ordination prayer from chapter 7 of Hippolytus's *Apostolic Tradition*, we read that the ordaining bishop prays, "Look upon this Your servant and impart the Spirit of grace and counsel of the presbyterate that he may help and govern Your people with a pure heart." Note that no mention is made of liturgizing, which was the function of the bishop. The presbyter was not primarily a liturgist. His task was one of "counsel," which he shared with the other presbyters, since the presbyterate is mentioned as a corporate and collegial reality. He was to "help" and "govern" along with his fellow presbyters.

The presbyters thus acted as counselors and advisors to the bishop. In what did their advice consist? In part, in deciding who was in or out of the church. This included decisions regarding whether or not a teacher should be expelled from the local community for teaching heresy; who might be ordained; and who might be reconciled to the community after excommunication.

Thus Noetus was expelled from Smyrna by the presbyters, not by the bishop alone, for the bishop could not depose a heretic by himself. When Bishop Alexander of Alexandria wanted to depose his presbyter Arius, he needed to call his fellow presbyters, even though Arius had already been condemned by a synod.[17] His clergy had a decisive role, not merely

---

17 Dix, *Jurisdiction in the Early Church* (London: Faith House, 1975), pp. 40–42.

a consultative one. When Cyprian appointed a subdeacon and a reader during a time of emergency without the express consent of his presbyters, he wrote to apologize and justify himself: "Nothing new has been done by me in your absence," he explains to them.[18] The presbyters' counsel was real and could not be lightly ignored. They were the bishop's indispensable advisors.

The bishop and his presbyters in fact formed a single governing body, with the presbyters judging and the bishop expressing this judgment through his liturgizing. We see this unity as early as Ignatius: "Your council of presbyters . . . is attuned to the bishop as strings to a lyre" (To the Eph. 4.1); "the deacon Zoticus . . . is subject to the bishop . . . and to the council of presbyters as to the law of Jesus Christ" (To the Magnes. 2); "Do nothing without the bishop, but be subject also to the council of presbyters" (To the Trall. 2.2); "You must follow the bishop as Jesus Christ followed the Father, and follow the council of presbyters as you would the apostles" (To the Smyrn. 8.1). In all Ignatius's letters, he takes care to join the authority of the bishop to that of the presbyters as constituting a single authority. Indeed, the bishop is called a "co-presbyter."

This unity, however, did not mean there was no distinction in their ministries. It was the bishop's task to lead and to be the guide of all, but guidance did not yet mean jurisdiction. This was the task of the presbyters. Thus the bishop in the

---

18 In his Epistle 23.

pre-Nicene Church had to consult his clergy and gain their assent in order to govern effectively. The bishop was the guide of all and took the initiative to lead. But power of unilateral decision was not yet his—this still rested with the presbyters as a whole. This is not to suggest that the bishop of the pre-Nicene Church was their mere tool. Being the chief liturgist and pastor, he usually got his way. But his was a moral authority among his people, not yet a juridical one. He could persuade but not command. The nature of his authority and of his working relationship with his presbyters is well illustrated in Cyprian's internal crisis with the lapsed of his church.

When the emperor Decius required everyone to offer sacrifice to the gods as part of his reform of the empire, a number of Christians did so, falling from the Faith and from membership in the Church. After offering the required sacrifice, the person was given a certificate declaring as much. Later some of these people repented and sought readmission to the church. The confessors (those who had suffered for the Faith, but had not been martyred) came to their aid and gave them a certificate, declaring that they had been readmitted to the church.

Cyprian viewed this as a bold usurpation of his own episcopal authority and as something entirely novel and without warrant. In one sense the confessor's action was completely traditional; it was the task of the presbyters to give judgment on such matters, and one tradition allowed confessors to function as presbyters by virtue of their suffering, even without actual ordination by the bishop.[19] Thus the confessors probably had no intention of innovating or of challenging their bishop's authority. As far as they were concerned, they were simply acting as governing presbyters had always acted, and perhaps expected their bishop would ratify what they had done.

Normally the bishop and his council of presbyters functioned as a unit, "as strings to a lyre," as Ignatius said. The presbyters (including the confessors) spoke and gave their counsel, and the bishop discerned the Word of the Lord, added his seal and blessing, and followed the counsel given. What mattered was not so much a strict division of powers and defined spheres of operation, but rather joint discernment of the Lord's will. The bishop might sway his presbyters if he disagreed with them, but this came from his moral authority and his ability to command respect as their chief shepherd and a man of God.

The problem Cyprian encountered with the lapsed and with the confessors was that it was just this moral authority he had compromised by his flight. As some saw it, their shepherd fled the persecution, leaving the rank and file of his flock to face the brunt of it alone, and the confessors now had more moral right to decide these things and discern the will of the Lord than their flighty bishop. Cyprian's problems illustrate the nature of the episcopal and presbyteral authority and show that legal

---

19 Thus Hippolytus's *Apostolic Tradition*, ch. 9: "A confessor, if he was in chains for the name of the Lord, shall not have hands laid on him for the diaconate or the presbyterate, for he has the honor of the presbyterate by his confession."

authority alone cannot carry the day. For the church leadership to function as it was meant to, bishop and presbyters needed to function together.

This presbyteral authority to govern and judge was expressed liturgically by the presbyters standing with the bishop at the altar during the Eucharist. He might have said the prayers, but they were also praying and consecrating. That was why, if increased numbers made a separate Eucharist in the city necessary, a presbyter could preside there. This possibility was as old as Ignatius, who wrote that a valid Eucharist was one under the bishop "or one to whom he shall have committed it" (To the Smyr. 8.1)—that is, to one of his fellow presbyters. The deacon might act only as the bishop's liturgical *assistant*, but the presbyter might act as his liturgical *deputy*, and this allowed him to serve in the city on his own.

This presbyteral deputed Eucharist was not a "rival altar" such as occurred in schism, because the celebrating presbyter acknowledged that he was under the local bishop as part of his team. As well as serving as the bishop's eucharistic deputy if need arose, the presbyters also functioned as teachers and as leaders of (noneucharistic) gatherings for prayer.

Sometimes, if a presbyter was known to be greatly skilled at teaching, his gifts were in demand beyond his local church. It was for that reason that Origen, though a presbyter, was invited to speak to the bishops gathered in council at Bostra, and the presbyter Malchion had a leading role at a council that deposed a bishop of Antioch in 269. For this latter, the conciliar letter was issued in the name of the bishops, presbyters, and deacons, and signed by the presbyters Malchion and Lucius, as well as by the bishops.[20] Though the bishops were the pastors of their sees, and as such were the usual participants at the regional councils, at this period they did not disdain the wisdom that was available through their presbyters.

Overview of the Pre-Nicene Episcopate

The leadership arrangement of the Church, from its origins in the first century to the end of the third century, was admirably fitted to fulfill its purpose of building up the local Christian community in love. The New Testament Church stressed mutual relationships and individual growth rooted in accountability and service. Thus Paul exhorted the Church, "Speak truth each one with his neighbor, for we are members of one another" (Eph. 4:25). The local body was supplied by these loving relationships and "held together by that which every joint supplies" (Eph. 4:16). Each was to "be subject to one another in the fear of Christ" (Eph. 5:21). Each one was to "regard one another with humility of mind as more important than yourself" so that they "maintain the same love, united in spirit, intent on one purpose" (Phil. 2:3, 2). They must "bear with one another, forgiving each other, whoever has a complaint against anyone . . . and let the peace of Christ rule in their hearts, to

---

20 Dix, *Jurisdiction*, op. cit., p. 57.

which indeed they were called in one body . . . with all wisdom teaching and admonishing one another with psalms, hymns, and spiritual songs" (Col. 3:13–16).

All these exhortations assume that the believers shared their personal lives together and felt they belonged to one another. The words "one another" recur like a refrain and witness to these deep connections. Leadership within these communities had as its goal the preservation and strengthening of these connections. Indeed, even the exalted ministries of apostles, prophets, evangelists, shepherds, and teachers had no other goal than "equipping the saints for the work of service, to the building up of the body of Christ," so that all in the community might "attain to the unity of the faith, to a mature man" (Eph. 4:11–13). The shepherds pastored, the presbyters ruled, solely to accomplish these aims among the rank and file.

The New Testament epistles thus provide a window into communities that were founded on mutual service and where relationships were paramount. The churches were not simply liturgical depots Christians visited for worship while they maintained their isolation from one another. Rather, the believers shared their lives in an intimate bond of brotherhood, finding in their communities "encouragement in Christ, consolation of love, fellowship of the Spirit, affection and love" (Phil. 2:1). The pre-Nicene leadership structure was admirably fitted to fulfill these goals of fellowship, which presupposed a community in which everyone could know his neighbor and relate closely to the bishop and his pastoral team. We note several characteristics of this leadership structure.

First of all, leadership was locally chosen. The faithful could more easily submit to the exhortation and admonishment of the pastors because they chose them. The faithful knew what sort of man their bishop would be, for he was not foisted upon them from without for reasons of political expediency that had nothing to do with them and their needs. Indeed, the consensus of the faithful in picking their new bishop was considered to be a sign that God also had chosen him, and this knowledge made it easier for them to submit to his pastoral rule.

Secondly, the episcopal authority was locally exercised. This means the bishop (and his presbyters) knew the pastoral situation and needs of the people for whom they would be making decisions. This reduced the likelihood of making inappropriate decisions, ones which did not fit with the local situation. Pastoral decisions needed to be rooted in intimate acquaintance with the local situation to be fruitful, and this acquaintance was scarcely possible if the bishop lived at a distance. Distant bishops might visit and participate in the ordination of the new bishop as a sign of wider catholicity. But they had nothing to say regarding the internal affairs of another see, one that was not their own local community.

This fierce independence of each local church was thus a pastoral necessity to save the local flock from the exercise of unwise pastoral authority. It was also the root of the bishop's authority to liturgize as he saw fit, for he needed the authority to tailor his liturgical praxis to meet local need. To know how to function liturgically, he needed to know the local situation. Thus each bishop in those days had his own anaphora, his own liturgical disciplines and praxis, and each bishop respected the integrity and independence of his neighbor.

The small and confined size of the bishop's see also acted as a kind of check on episcopal leadership, for if the bishop made unpopular decisions, he could not hide from their consequences but had to face his people every Sunday and endure their opprobrium. He could not thunder at them from on high, for he did not live on high but in the midst of his people. He would see their faces up close every Sunday when he administered the Eucharist to them. This intimate quality of the pastoral relationship helped keep the shepherd accountable to his flock.

Thirdly, because all pastoral work was done as part of a team of presbyters, each presbyter had less opportunity to err, since he worked closely with others who could rebuke and correct him. It was harder for them to hide, being part of a college that consulted often and worshipped together every week. The positive side of this team ministry and plurality of local presbyters meant that no shepherd suffered isolation or loneliness. The presence of other presbyters nearby, living in the same city and sitting together in church, meant that each one was supported by the others. The clergy could gain strength from one another, since no one labored alone. The older ones could mentor the younger ones and provide an ongoing pastoral education.

Fourthly, the permanence of the appointment meant problems between pastor and flock had to be worked out, for the option of dealing with problems by waiting for the pastor's eventual replacement could not arise. The bishop was not present in his see as a temporary placement, as one rung of a ladder, as one step in a career. Once elected and ordained, the clergyman was there for life, with no possibility of retirement or transfer. Permanency of placement meant he could function in his see as the father to a family, and this in turn meant a better chance for the laity to relate to one another as to brothers and sisters. Everyone could thus feel they belonged to one another and become a true family in Christ.

Many of these advantages would be increasingly imperiled and lost in the times to come, as we shall see when we examine the changes that occurred in the fourth century.

THE CHANGE IN THE FOURTH CENTURY
An Emerging Elite

WHEN THE THIRD CENTURY gave place to the fourth, no one could have foreseen what lay ahead. The emperor Diocletian, though an able and brilliant organizer, had waged a relentless war on the Church in a determined attempt to check the dangerous spread of Christianity. It is easy to demonize Diocletian and to view him simply as a bloodthirsty persecutor. It is therefore all the more important to place him (and therefore his persecution) in context.

Throughout the second and third centuries, Rome had to deal with ever-escalating financial difficulties as the empire grew, and it dealt with them by tightening its imperial grip on the cities. When Diocletian undertook to deal with this financial crisis, the state's authority became paramount. He was determined to break the power of the Church, for he judged it to be a state within the state, and as such a clear threat to the Roman state's authority and ability to deal adequately with the crisis. Diocletian's goal was to save the empire and return it if possible to its former glory, and that meant not just the supremacy of Rome itself, but the supremacy of her gods as well. For both civil and religious reasons, therefore, the Christians stood in the way of his policies aimed at rescuing the empire from disaster. Diocletian unleashed a savage persecution on the Church that raged from 303–311, one of such intensity that it nearly wiped the Church out.

That persecution came to an end with the Edict of Toleration issued by Galerius as he lay in his final agonies, and Constantine's confirmation of this policy in 313. This did not make Christianity the state Church, nor even the official and mandated religion of the empire. This would come later, under the emperors Theodosius and Justinian. Constantine pursued a more pluralistic policy. Under his rule, the law said that "no man should be denied leave of attaching himself to the rites of Christians or to whatever other religion his mind directed him . . . the open and free exercise of their respective religions is granted to all others, as well as to the Christians . . . and we mean not to derogate anything from the honor due to any religion or its votaries."

But although freedom was granted to all, Constantine

favored the Christians and made no secret of his attachment to their beliefs. He restored their confiscated property and favored them by building churches funded by the imperial treasury. For the Christians who had been savagely hounded by his predecessor, it was almost too good to believe. An earthquake had occurred, and everything seemed to have been moved out of its long-accustomed place. Constantine seemed to be a walking miracle. But the miracle came with a price tag.

The Constantinian Earthquake

One can overstate the effect Constantine had on the Church, and a certain kind of confessional polemics indeed made Constantine almost a symbol for everything considerable objectionable in the Church forever after. These polemics presuppose that as soon as Constantine began to favor the Christians, suddenly everyone in the Church lost his or her integrity. The truth is much more complicated and nuanced. It is true that with Constantine things began to change, but that change was gradual.

Constantine had "come out" as a Christian, and he sincerely tried to favor the Christians and help them fulfill their divine calling. It is safe to say he found it frustrating at times, with Christian groups quarreling and excommunicating one another. As well as a genuine concern for the unity of the Church on spiritual grounds (shared by all Christians), he needed the Church to be united if it was to fulfill his vision of one God, one empire, one Church. That is, he wanted to favor Christ's Church, and so he needed to know which of the many competing groups claiming to be the Church was actually the Church. And one can, after all, see his point.

The Church was slow to grasp what all this meant, perhaps because the change was too great to foresee all its eventual consequences immediately. A complete inner revolution was required of Christians in the early fourth century. At the end of the third century, it was taken for granted that the Roman empire was the enemy, the Great Satan—or, to be more biblically precise, the great Dragon that waged war against the saints, the Beast with seven heads, Babylon the Great, mother of harlots and abominations of the earth (Rev. 12:3; 13:1; 17:5). Christians had always prayed for the emperor and for the empire, but the best thing that could be said about them was that they prevented worse evil and chaos, and that while Rome and its emperor stood, the Antichrist was not yet able to come. Now, a few years later, the impossible had happened—Caesar had converted to Christ while remaining Caesar. Suddenly the world was no longer the arena in which they were persecuted and slaughtered, but the mission field in which they were bidden to reap the field white for harvest. It took some getting used to.

The Church was now called upon to interact with the emperor, to speak with one united voice, to make judgments and function as the conscience of the world. It was just here that the Church found itself initially unequal to the task. As we saw above, in the second and third centuries the churches were organized into tightly autonomous communities. They possessed some machinery for joint action, but not much. Bishops met with other bishops periodically. Bishops of large sees exercised their local primacies and gave advice, direction, and sometimes intervention. Bishops would meet in councils to decide what to do about emerging heresies or pastoral problems, or to discuss liturgical questions.

But in that time there was no mechanism of enforcement, and if a particular community chose to defy neighboring bishops or primates or councils, there was little anyone else could do as long as the people of the defiant church stood by their bishop. This independence meant the whole Church could not be crushed by the persecuting empire at a stroke; there was no single head or institution that could be destroyed so as to give the Church at large a death blow. There was nothing in the early Church resembling the centralized imperial administration, no machinery by which the Church could discuss things, know its own mind, and take thoughtful corporate action in response to the new situation. It was organized effectively only on the local level; there was no effective higher organization by which it could make a concerted response to the empire. It was into this vacuum that Constantine stepped.

The problems arose when the emperor began consistently to act in the only way possible for an emperor to act—namely, imperially. When the emperor put the machinery of the state at the service of the Church, that machinery functioned very differently from the pre-Nicene machinery of the Church. To take one example out of many: the determination of which was the true Church in event of schism. The emperor wanted to favor the true Church and so wanted to determine which group *was* the true Church. He bade the Church hold councils, and when the dissident groups got the worst of it at the councils and would not abide by the council's decision, he stepped in to enforce the conciliar decision himself, with force of arms if necessary.

The imperial machinery was created to be efficient and quick. But this was contrary to the way things were done in the pre-Nicene Church. The Church in those days possessed no machinery of enforcement, so that if two rival groups fought, each would excommunicate the other and live separately. One group would thrive, and the other would eventually die out. It thus might take a generation or two to see where the truth lay and discern which church's claims were true, but the faithful would eventually work things out over time. That was fine for then, and it worked.

But in the new imperial oversight of the Church, it was not fine, for the emperor needed to know *now* where the truth lay. Earlier, the Church's task was simply to *proclaim* the truth. Now the State was prepared to *enforce* it. The result in the fourth century was a series of Arian and Arianizing councils with the emperor siding first with this group and then with that.[21] Athanasius was banished five times by the emperor, for the imperial machinery was very efficient.[22] The church's cooperation with the emperor would yield much good fruit in the following years and centuries. But the Byzantine experiment would produce some bitter fruit as well.

Changes in the Local Leadership in the Fourth Century

The Church strove to play catch-up with the new situation in which it found itself as well as it could. Not having the necessary administrative machinery to deal with the empire, it let the emperor lead. But it soon enough began to take its cue from the emperor and develop machinery of its own. It took the borders of the empire to be its own borders. The Church created its own trans-local structures, incorporating the old primacies (such as Rome and Alexandria) into a newer, more organized system.

---

21 The Church's struggle with Arianism also served to increase the importance of the bishop's office, for the local faithful as well as the other churches of the area would only remain in communion with a church if its bishop confessed the correct faith. Note: It was the confession *of the bishop*, not (for example) of his presbyters, that determined the acceptability of his church to other churches—and of course, to the emperor. The local church's orthodoxy hung on the orthodoxy of its bishop, and this could not fail to increase the importance of the office.

22 This does not mean of course that the Church of that era was a hotbed of heresy and schism, but simply that history of necessity focuses its narrative upon the exciting and sensational.

The senior bishop of the area was now the bishop of the civil capital of the province, regardless of his actual seniority. The eparchy was a grouping of provinces, and the patriarchates corresponded to the praetorian prefectures.[23] Local regional councils began to be prescribed, not just to deal with heresies or schisms (which did not often arise), but also to deal with potential difficulties of discipline, such as whether or not to kneel for prayer on Sunday. (Consistent attendance at these local councils was a hard sell; the canonical prescription needed to be continually repeated.) Canonical collections began to be produced. In all these developments, the Church of the fourth century was striving to create a way by which it could know its own mind on a wider scale. The old pre-Nicene local autonomy and independence was felt to be a hindrance in meeting the needs of the times.

One of the first things that happened in the fourth century was a spectacular growth in numbers of those seeking identification with the Christian faith. It would be unkind as well as inaccurate to think the Church lost her head and simply baptized everyone that came her way without making efforts to ensure the candidate's motives were true. It strengthened the system of its catechumenate, including a series of "scrutinies" that looked at the life of the potential convert, with sponsors required to bear witness in public to the candidate's pure life. The fact that some preferred to defer baptism until their

---

23 Dix, "Ministry in the Early Church," op. cit., p. 276.

deathbed, though denounced by some pastors, at least showed the average person understood that a higher standard was required of them than before. The Church also kept up an efficient penitential system, excommunicating offenders for what appears to us moderns as a very long time.

All these provisions witness to the fact that the fourth-century church at least tried its best to uphold the old pre-Nicene standards. This growth in numbers meant it was increasingly difficult to contain all the Christians in a city under one roof for the single episcopal Eucharist.

Change for the Presbyters

This also meant a change in the office of the presbyter, for before the numerical growth in large city churches, the presbyter in those churches had no special liturgical role. The bishop liturgized, and the presbyters simply stood by as a college and prayed silently, for offering prayer aloud was the role of the bishop.

Now more presbyters began to preside in the other eucharistic assemblies in the city near the bishop's Eucharist, and thus they also now had a liturgical role. More and more presbyters came to be seen as men whose task it was not simply to rule as part of a college, but to preside at Eucharists of their own—though doubtless their traditional role of teaching at the weekday gatherings throughout the city prepared the way for them in their new role of presiding there at the Sunday Eucharist.

This meant the link that bound presbyters to the bishop was increasingly strained. Formerly, people viewed presbyters not as individuals with power to offer the Eucharist, but mainly as members of the bishop's college of advisors. Now the people came more and more to view presbyters as eucharistic celebrants *in their own right*. Certainly the presbyters had always had the ability to preside if necessary. But the point is that this presidency was unusual and only done *if necessary*; now it is taken to be the norm.

By the time of St. Jerome in the West (who died in 420), the liturgical roles of bishop and presbyter would be considered as essentially the same, so that Jerome could ask rhetorically, "What function, except ordination, belongs to a bishop that does not also belong to a presbyter?" Chrysostom in the East thought the same: "Between presbyters and bishops there was no great difference. For [bishops] are only superior in having the power of ordination."[24] In former days, the presbyter was not considered as having a personal consecratory power that he could exercise on his own. His new role as eucharistic consecrator meant that increasingly he came to be seen as a man with power to consecrate *as his main task*.

In the late fourth century, the older liturgical materials were amended to reflect this new role, so that to the original prayer for the ordination of a presbyter from Hippolytus's *Apostolic Tradition* was added the phrase "that he may perform the

---

24 Jerome, Epistle 146; Chrysostom, Homily 11 on 1 Timothy.

spotless sacred rites on behalf of Your people"—that is, offer the Eucharist. This revision process extended to a reissuing of the old Epistles of St. Ignatius, wherein the term "priest" is now applied to the presbyter.[25] Formerly it was only the bishop who was called "priest" by virtue of his task of liturgizing and offering the eucharistic Sacrifice. With the usual deputation of this eucharistic presidency to the presbyter, the language of priesthood becomes attached to him also.

As the presbyter came to be seen as the normal celebrant of the Eucharist, a shift in the role of deacons occurred also. Formerly, the deacon was fundamentally the assistant of the bishop. In discussing deacons, Hippolytus's *Apostolic Tradition* says, "In the ordination of a deacon, the bishop alone shall lay on hands, because [the deacon] is not being ordained to the priesthood, but to the service of the bishop, to do what is ordered by him."[26] So close was the relation of deacon to bishop that archdeacons were often elected to succeed their bishops when the latter died. Yet by the late fourth century, deacons are scattered throughout the cities in which they serve, no longer for the service of the bishop, but as liturgical assistants to the presbyters. This alone speaks volumes about the presbyteral takeover of the bishop's former role.

The bishop therefore no longer regarded the presbyters as his advisory council, but as his deputies. They did not serve with

---

25 Zizioulas, *Eucharist, Bishop, Church* (Brookline: Holy Cross Press, 2001), p. 205.
26 *Apostolic Tradition*, chapter 8.

him at the Eucharist, standing alongside and fulfilling a pastoral function to the same community the bishop served. Instead, they were increasingly sent by him and left his side to go and preside at the Eucharists of other communities. This meant the breakup of the old episcopal unity expressed in the Eucharist and the growth of many presbyteral Eucharists, which in fact came to be regarded as the norm. This may have seemed like a promotion of the presbyters to a more important task, but it had other far-reaching results for the bishop's role as well.

Change for the Bishop

As the presbyters assumed a role less tied to and defined by their relationship with their local bishop, the bishop also became increasingly free from accountability to the local presbyterate. In the third century, the bishop did not possess administrative power to command, but had to seek the assent of his presbyteral council. In the fourth century, as the presbyters became less his advising council and more his deputies, the bishop became increasingly free from the necessity of obtaining their assent to his decisions. Now matters of policy lay with him alone.

The bishop has gone from being president of a gathered community to being the ruler of a territorial diocese. One detects a new confidence on the part of the bishops in their decision making. They are now the elite. They no longer exercise authority *in* the church, but *over* it. Theirs is now no longer the *moral* authority of prophet and man of God, but a *juridical* authority of one in charge of a vast organization.

If his presbyters experienced a "promotion" in their ability to normatively celebrate the Eucharist apart from their bishop, the bishop also experienced such a promotion, in that he was increasingly free from the necessity of consulting his presbyters. This change was furthered by the proliferation of episcopal councils, mandated to be held twice a year. The Council of Nicea, for example, decreed this in canon 5:

> Concerning those who have been excommunicated, either among the clergy or the laity, let the sentence that was given by the bishops of each province remain in force; let this be in conformity with the regulation which requires that those so excluded by some bishops must not be received by others. But let each case be examined to see if those involved were excluded for a cowardly reason, from a quarrelsome spirit, or from some feeling of dislike on the part of the bishop. Therefore, so that a proper inquiry may take place, it seems good and proper that in each province there be a synod two times a year so that all the bishops of the province sitting together may examine such questions and thus those who, according to the general opinion, may have disobeyed their bishop will be properly considered as excommunicate by all until such time as all the bishops see fit to render a more merciful sentence. Let the synods be held as follows: one before the fortieth day [i.e., before Lent] . . . the second during the fall.

We note several things in this canon. The first is that bishops are to meet together twice a year to discuss matters and arrive at a consensus concerning questions of common interest. Nicea was not alone in this. The Council of Antioch also decreed in canon 20, "As is required by the needs of the church ... it seems good and proper that the bishops of the province come together in a synod twice a year: the first time after the third week that follows Pascha ... the second synod will take place at the *ides* of October." The so-called "Apostolic Canons," dating from about this time, also decreed (canon 37), "Let there be a meeting of the bishops twice a year, and let them examine among themselves the decrees concerning religion and settle the church controversies which may have occurred."

The holding of regular councils was in the fourth-century air as a revolutionary new norm. The pre-Nicene Church always possessed within itself a universal spirit and a consciousness of being spread throughout the world, and the bishops always viewed themselves as collectively sharing the entire episcopate. But this does not explain why the Church did not do more to meet together in council before the fourth century. It is true that persecution made such meetings difficult, but the bishops still managed to meet together sometimes for ordinations of bishops. If councils were so crucial to the Church's life in the pre-Nicene period, why did the bishops not meet for small councils when they met for ordinations?

The fact that the councils were not only held often in the

fourth century, but that they were *mandated* to be held often, witnesses to something revolutionary. The local church's pre-Nicene independence, for good or for ill (or both), was being eroded. No doubt this occurred because the bishops of that time perceived a new need. The local churches needed to take united and concerted action, and interchurch unity became more important. That is what lies behind the words "as is required by the needs of the church" in canon 20 of the Council of Antioch. Before this time, the needs of the Church did not require such meetings.

These canons thus subject the autonomy of the local church in a way that was new. Before the fourth century, there was still discipline among bishops, and the idea that a man excommunicated in one local church should not be blithely received in another was in force. This is taken for granted in canon 5 of Nicea and treated as something customary. But the spirit with which questions are treated has changed, and now the councils will enforce such things. It is now accepted as natural ("good and proper") that local decisions be subjected to a more general inquiry, so that the autonomy of the local bishop has been decreased. Admittedly, there is still no machinery of enforcement, and refusal to uphold another bishop's sentence of excommunication was still possible if the defiant church was determined to go its own way. But everyone now seemed to acknowledge that such independence was no longer helpful. The bishops were prepared to subject their former independence to the synods, even if it meant their original sentence would be overturned.

Further, we must not miss the fact that these provisions for regular provincial synods of bishops not only limit the local authority of bishops, but practically eradicate the authority of the local presbyters. The councils were taking on the right to override local decisions. For in the pre-Nicene Church, the responsibility for excommunication lay with the presbyters. Now their decisions can be overturned not just by their own bishop, but by a gathering of bishops *from other cities*. Their own presbyteral authority to decide these matters has been completely set aside. And, more significantly, *the authority of the local church* has been set aside, and this in favor of the authority of the wider Church, acting through synods of bishops. The bishop was becoming the local representative of a large organization rather than the center of his local community.

This means the local bishop no longer regarded himself as subject to his presbyters and his people, but as subject to a synod of bishops. Formerly, when a bishop met with other bishops, he attended as a representative of his own church, to express its voice and mind to the other churches. Now things have changed, so that when the bishop meets with other bishops, he returns home to convey the decisions of the synod to his people. The controlling center has shifted from the local church to the synod, and the bishop, formerly the church's representative *to the synod*, now has become the synod's representative *to* the local church. It seems as if the bishops of the fourth century welcomed the increase of their personal power. They preferred the distant and more theoretical control of a synod to the close and practical control of presbyters and people.

The new emphasis on episcopal power meant that transfers of bishops to more prestigious sees were bound to increase—though all for the good of the Church, of course. Once the concept of a bishop belonging primarily to the wider Church gained ground at the expense of the concept of his being wed to his local community, such transfers and promotions were inevitable, especially since now being bishop of a large church could have many rewards. Before, being the bishop of a large church meant increased visibility to the persecuting authorities and therefore increased chance of martyrdom. In that situation, being bishop of a small backwater town where one could better keep one's head down had its attractions. But no longer. Now the larger sees were more attractive.

That meant, inevitably, that the attractive sees drew some unattractive men. The new system tended to stress the bishop's administrative role over his pastoral one. The bishop of the fourth century begins to come into his own as the new elite of a Church called to function in a new world.

Overview of the Post-Nicene Episcopate

It is easy to be critical of the changes that occurred in the leadership structure in the fourth century. Many people have blamed the leadership during the days of Constantine, thinking it should have resisted what later generations have called the caesaropapism of the emperor and imperial control of the Church. But in the fourth century, it would have required supernatural foresight to see how Constantine would be succeeded by Justinian and Theodosius, and just how closely state and Church would become enmeshed, and what kind of symphony would actually be produced by the Byzantine harmony of emperor and patriarch. Indeed, many at the time thought the imperial favor of Constantine would simply prove to be a passing fad, a flash in the imperial pan, and that after him the tide would not turn, but return to its wonted flow. The rule of the emperor Julian the Apostate seemed for a time to confirm this pessimistic forecast. But the Christians of the fourth century happily took what they could get for as long as it lasted.

And anyway, what could they have done even if they had wanted to resist the imperial "help" of Constantine? The Church had been nearly wiped out in the last century by Diocletian's policies, and no one wanted to return to the old times. Besides, the pre-Nicene discipline and church machinery only involved people who were actually baptized and who submitted themselves to its discipline and machinery, and Constantine was officially not yet even a catechumen. How could they have stood in his path, even if they chose to? All the authority and initiative lay with Constantine. The Church responded to Constantine as it had responded to the state throughout its existence—namely, with passivity. The state acted, and the Church coped with its actions as best as it could.

Of course there were gains. The pre-Nicene Church, for all the persecution it endured, never stopped doing evangelism and trying to convert as many people to the Faith as possible. Here were unprecedented opportunities for fulfilling its apostolic mandate. The floods of people coming to the Church were viewed by the bishops of the fourth century not as a threat to the Church's purity, but as souls for whom Christ died and who needed to be saved in the cleansing waters of baptism. More than this, the new Constantinian situation meant the Church could more fully fulfill its divine mission of helping the poor, and the work of bishops like Basil the Great testifies to how well it fulfilled that mission. It seemed in the fourth century that Caesar and his empire wanted to make a prostration before the cross of Christ—who were the bishops to say they couldn't?

Having made due allowance for why the bishops of the fourth century acted as they did, we note that the leadership structure of the Church underwent drastic alteration. In particular, it seems the bishop and his presbyters swapped roles. The bishop of the pre-Nicene Church was primarily a liturgist, and his presbyters were primarily administrators. Now the bishop functioned increasingly as an administrator, and his presbyters functioned as the main liturgists and celebrants of the Eucharist. The presbyteral parish was replacing the episcopal cathedral as the place where the rank and file received the Eucharist.

The bishop, formerly everyone's pastor in the local church, was becoming the administrator of a vast enterprise. The change was gradual enough, but it was destined to continue and grow.

As the distance between the bishop and his presbyters continued to grow, the bishop's accountability to them and to his local church continued correspondingly to diminish. Previously, the bishop had to decide his policy with an eye to making it work in his local church through the power of his moral authority. Now he could depend on his canonical or constitutional authority to carry the day, even apart from his personal gifts. The presbyters, whose counsel was once sought, now were simply his deputies and messengers. As the bishop's accountability gravitated more and more to the provincial councils of bishops (which he might or might not actually have attended; non-attendance was the reason the canon had to be repeated so often in church history), he could act more autocratically in his local church. This meant the opportunities for tension and problems increased as well.

The same could be said of the presbyters of the fourth century. Previously they were accountable to their bishop and to each other. Now that the presbyter was increasingly more a parish priest than a member of a group, he also found himself less encumbered by accountability. The presbyteral assumption of eucharistic presidency meant a promotion in the eyes of many. It also meant that each presbyter had more independence from the other presbyters and from his bishop. Once again, this new arrangement made for more opportunities for tension and power struggle between clergy. Also, it planted the seed of isolation for the parish priest now that he was no longer a member of a team. The seed would grow to produce the dry fruit of loneliness in the centuries to come.

Further, the new arrangement meant bishops could be more easily transferred, even if for a while the old aversion to such transfers remained. The people increasingly felt less connected to their bishop and had less pastoral association with him. In many places, it was no longer the bishop who baptized and anointed them and fed them the weekly Eucharist, but their own presbyter. The intimate bonds that united bishop, presbyters, and people in one indissoluble family were coming unraveled.

This was all the more the case when bishops were transferred to another see. In the pre-Nicene Church, both election and ordination were considered indispensable to create a bishop. Now ordination alone was required. The people's new bishop might no longer be the man they knew intimately and had chosen to be their pastor, and as the fourth century progressed, the role of the people in electing bishops all but disappeared. An episcopal appointment might be the result of imperial choice or of the new bishop's own ambition. This could not but diminish the emotional connection people felt for their chief shepherd.

In short, the major change in leadership of the Church in the fourth century was that it was slowly replacing *organism* with *hierarchy*. The pre-Nicene Church functioned as an organism, with each person in the local community exercising his gift for the common good (as in the Pauline metaphor described in 1 Cor. 12:7f). Certain gifts were more prominent (such as the gift of bishop or presbyter), but all members of the Church made their own essential contribution.

The laity, for example, made the essential contribution of electing their new bishop and by their consensus revealing the candidate to be the divine choice. The presbyters co-consecrated the Eucharist with their bishop, for when the eucharistic Gifts were offered to the bishop, the bishop laid his hands upon it "with all the presbytery" (*Ap. Trad.* ch. 4). The presbyters shared in the ordination of a new presbyter, touching the new candidate even as the bishop laid hands upon him (*Ap. Trad.* ch. 7). In the words of the author of *Apostolic Tradition*, the bishop ordains, while the presbyters seal what the bishop does (*Ap. Trad.* ch. 8). Everyone has his part to play, just as all members of the body are necessary to its proper functioning. The eye could not say to the hand, "I have no need of you" (1 Cor. 12:21), nor could the bishop say to the presbyter, "I have no need of you." Each function was equally valued, because all functions were essential to the health of the local church.

This began to change in the fourth century, as the bishop increasingly said to the presbyter, "I have no need of you." Why rely upon the presbyters when you could have other bishops—or the emperor? With the replacement of organism with hierarchy, other functions become "lower" functions, and the offices of reader, exorcist, deacon, and presbyter are now arranged in order of importance and sanctity.

We see the final form of this process in the works of (Pseudo) Dionysius. In this system, the shepherd has become "the hierarch," and the arrangement of church offices on Earth mirrors the arrangement of the angelic hosts in heaven. An archangel is closer to God than an angel, just as a bishop is closer to God than a presbyter or a deacon. Hierarchy (or clericalism, to give it its other name) allowed one to locate sanctity not in the local church as a whole, but in the bishop (or at least in the clergy).

One begins at this time to see the bishops looking down on the presbyters. In the pre-Nicene Church, the bishops did not scruple to invite the great presbyter Origen to teach. Now bishops could scoff at the idea that a bishop could be misled by a lowly presbyter: when some bishops met in Antioch in 341, they wrote to Pope Julius of Rome, defending themselves against charges of Arianism by saying, "We have neither been followers of Arius, for how should we as bishops follow a presbyter?"[27] By now, any thought that a bishop would follow a presbyter's counsel is considered unworthy and impossible. One gets the impression that the Fathers gathered in Antioch could not decide which was the more outrageous, the idea of them following a heretic or the idea of them following a presbyter.

In this new system of hierarchy (or "hierarchicalism," if one

---

27 As cited in John Behr's *The Nicene Faith, Part 1* (Crestwood: SVS Press, 2004), p. 24.

prefers) the thought took root that each order was higher than the previous one and to some degree contained the previous one. Instead of viewing the diaconate, for example, as a ministry in itself, it was increasingly understood that deacons were arranged under and were lower than presbyters, but were above readers. The presbyters were below bishops, but above deacons. The pre-Nicene concept of each order or task having its own inherent dignity was giving way to the concept that some orders were higher than others. The pre-Nicene Church accordingly would ordain a layman (like Cyprian of Carthage) to the episcopate immediately, without ordaining him first as deacon and presbyter, if he were elected; latter ages would insist that the elected lay candidate pass through all the ordinations, such as deacon and presbyter, before being ordained to the episcopate (such as in the case of Ambrose of Milan).[28] *Differences* of ministry mutated into *levels* of ministry, with the episcopate being the highest "level."

In this system and mentality, it was inevitable that the laity be demoted. In the Dionysian ladder of sanctity, they were at the bottom rung, with nothing to give and everything to receive. To be part of the laity in the pre-Nicene Church meant to be part of the holy and privileged People of God (Gr. *laos*), the chosen race, the holy nation, the royal priesthood (1 Pet. 2:9). Pagans and even catechumens were the outsiders; the *laos* were the insiders, the initiated, the ones with the privilege of

---

28 Ibid., p. 284.

receiving the Body and Blood of Christ, the ones whose liturgical "Amen" was required at all the public prayers of the Church, the ones whose voice and vote were essential in the election and creation of bishops. The catechumens were not allowed to give the kiss of peace at the Eucharist "because their kiss was not holy."[29] The laity, however, could give the kiss, because their kiss *was* holy. For the author of the *Apostolic Tradition*, the laity and clergy to whom the work was addressed were quite capable of making correct pastoral judgments when required, "for we all have the Spirit of God."[30] Note: All the people possessed the Spirit of God, not just the clergy.

This perception would be eroded increasingly beginning in the fourth century. Under the new system, the laity were considered not as the initiated, but as the *un*initiated. It was but a short step before they lost the glow of their original sanctity as well, and by the fifth century, the term *laikos* came to mean little more than "profane." Formerly the Eucharist was done *by* them, as the concerted act of clergy and laity working together. Now it is done *for* them, by the clergy, and their task is simply to receive what they are given. This demoted place of the laity and the new passivity would take time to influence the Church's liturgy. But it would come soon enough. By the middle of the sixth century, the emperor Justinian would have to order that the anaphora be chanted loud enough to be heard by the people.

---

29 *Apostolic Tradition*, ch. 18.
30 Ibid., ch. 16.

Even then, Justinian gives as his reason "so that hearing, their hearts may be moved to greater devotion and praise of God." It seems not to occur to anyone that the people need to hear the prayer so that they can seal it with their "Amen." The laity are no longer on the list of indispensable players at the Eucharist.

The replacement of the concept of organism with that of hierarchicalism took time, and it seems to have happened so gradually that it went largely unnoticed. The people's attention was too taken up with the new opportunities of the moment and with the miracle of an emperor turned Christian to much notice the subtle change in church leadership. After all, nothing constitutionally had changed, for the bishop was still the head of the local church, and he still served the Eucharist at his cathedral, attended by presbyters and deacons. The presbyter was increasingly becoming the parish priest, but the people were used to presbyters presiding at weekday services for teaching and prayer, and even presiding at the Eucharist in larger cities when necessary. And it took time for the newly rooted plant to blossom and bear its clericalist fruit.

Of course, clericalist fruit was not the only kind of fruit it produced. The bishop also bore the fruit of good works, charitable foundations, and other forms of philanthropic institutions. Like the great and wealthy men of old, they gave plenty of benefactions and were called "benefactors" (Luke 22:25). The change of situation wasn't all bad. It is to the good works and the lives of the bishops in that changed situation that we now turn.

CHAPTER FOUR

THE BISHOP IN THE FOURTH CENTURY
The Patron of the City

IN THE BRIGHT WORLD that was emerging Byzantium, it was a good time to be a Christian (and a bad time, honesty compels us to add, to be a heretic). The cross of Christ was exalted over all, and the Church was growing as never before. Temples were being built and adorned, some in grand fashion. Money was flowing freely, and in the center of all this wonderful activity was the person of the bishop.

The Bishop as Man about Town

The task of the bishop in the wider society paralleled those of any of the upper classes and landowners. The *patronus* or public benefactor was expected to use his wealth to help others, providing food in times of famine, constructing buildings, roads, public baths, aqueducts, and temples, and putting on public games and entertainments. The bishop, as one having access to the rich resources of his church, also provided for the poor and orphans and built churches, chapels, and monasteries, as well as ransoming slaves and interceding with the higher authorities if need be.

This happened not because the bishops had been co-opted by the state and absorbed into the secular social structure. The bishops had always worked to fulfill the goals of helping the poor and being socially conscious, so this role was nothing new for them. The bishop's responsibilities listed in the *Didascalia*, reflecting earlier traditions, included helping widows, orphans, the poor, and strangers. Indeed, bishops had been known to intercede with the emperor on behalf of the needy even *before* Constantine. What was new was the scope the new Constantinian situation allowed for their action.

As the Church grew in influence and as the old and wealthy families concluded Christianity was here to stay, many from the municipal elite started to find in the episcopate a good career option. Indeed, the landowners were the largest recruiting ground for the clergy. There was a degree of permeability between secular civic office and ecclesiastical office. Upwardly mobile men with long and good careers in the civil service would leave their secular occupations to join the Church (thus proving, by the way, that those attaching themselves to the

Church were not simply motivated by careerism and a desire for advancement), and those with successful careers in the Church would also later seek civil office.[31]

This latter would cause some concern to the Church, which dealt with it in conciliar legislation (see Council of Chalcedon, canon 7: "those who have been admitted into the ranks of the clergy must no longer accept any secular dignity"). The existence of such legislation, of course, witnessed to how widespread the practice was. The Church could protest that bishops were accepting "secular dignity." The fact was that *the office of bishop itself* was now becoming a secular dignity, so that the line between civic honor and ecclesiastical honor was becoming blurred. It is not surprising then if some of the clergy found the line difficult to draw.

The dividing line between civic and ecclesiastical was all the harder to see since the virtues required of both bishop and civic leader were often indistinguishable. The civic patron was praised for his "meekness," as was the Christian bishop. The ideal patron was to be meek or gentle, but gentle in the sense of being "a true gentleman," someone gallant, kind to the poor and destitute. It is significant that the term was applied also to Moses, the archetypical model for the man of God, described in Numbers 12:3 as "very meek, more than any man who was on the face of the earth." The word for "meek" in the Septuagint

---

31 Much of the material in this chapter is drawn from Claudia Rapp, *Holy Bishops in Late Antiquity* (Los Angeles: Univ. of California Press, 2005).

of this passage is *praus*. Thus Moses, the civic-minded Roman landowner, and the Christian bishop were united by the same ancient virtue, showing that the line between civic and Christian virtue was thinly drawn, especially in the minds of most people in the fourth century. The very duties to which the landowners felt themselves obliged were often the same ones that were the bishop's characteristic social responsibility.

The common people—those who stood to gain the most by the bishop's patronage and public benefactions—understood this clearly. That is why they wanted and consistently chose for their bishops men of breeding, wealth, and influence. It seems that for many of the rank and file, this social prominence counted for more than the holiness of the candidate.

An example of such a bishop is Synesius, bishop of Ptolemais. He was born around 370 in North Africa to a wealthy landowning family. He had a successful secular career and a proven track record in the civil service, was married, and was perhaps as much Neoplatonist as Christian. It is significant that when the people wanted to elect him for their bishop in 411, he consented, after great hesitation, on two conditions. He would cease his hobbies of hunting, sport, and time for private study, but two things he would not give up. One was his wife. He demanded that he be allowed to keep her openly and not be forced to hide her away in secret. "On the contrary," he said, "I want many, well-bred children"—and this in a time when celibacy was increasingly encouraged. The second condition was that he not be forced to renounce his Neoplatonic philosophy. He agreed to "speak mythologically" while in public, as his episcopal duties required, but he would not say anything with which he sincerely disagreed.

Despite these conditions, the people still demanded him as their bishop, thinking that a person of such worldly experience and prestige would be a great adornment for their church. They judged that his ability to be a good patron was more important than his personal beliefs. (To his credit, it may be said that once ordained bishop, he fulfilled this task as conscientiously as he fulfilled his previous civic tasks, even excommunicating a cruel and greedy governor who was oppressing the people.)

Synesius's case revealed what the people of the fourth century wanted in a bishop and what the Church required as it dealt with the wider world. The bishop had become a patron for his city, one of its civic leaders, and was valued for his ability to give to others. The Lord's teaching, "It is more blessed to give than to receive" (Acts 20:35), now became the favorite verse of the people and the most valued function of the bishop. The poor but pious laborer who might earlier, during the pre-Nicene era, have been chosen as bishop by his community because of his holiness now had little chance of becoming bishop. Bigger and richer men had pushed him out of the way. It was taken for granted by some that men of good social standing would be ordained. Accordingly, those who were *not* of good social standing found a glass ceiling when it came to promotion in the Church.

The office of bishop was now a socially valuable commodity. That is, it was coveted by many and (sometimes) sold. Members of the landowning class who competed for municipal offices and their honors now cast their eyes on the episcopal office as well, perhaps attracted by the wealth bishops had and could command as much as by the public honor that accrued from the office. They would use their connections with powerful civic leaders to help them secure the job.

Some were not above trying to buy the office—or at least greasing a number of palms to help secure their election. Obviously, the Church at large rejected such a procedure as the sin of simony and outlawed it with severe penalties, declaring the bishop's ordination null and void as well as the ordinations later done by him. But the canons outlawing the practice point to the fact that it was widespread. And it was perhaps less easy to prove than might be imagined. Like a true and generous patron, the newly appointed bishop gave gifts to his clergy, in proportion to how much money he had access to, and this was considered as the usual custom. The giving of the bribe money after the election to those who elected the new bishop was thus difficult to separate from the giving of the customary gifts. This meant, of course, that candidates of more limited financial means had even less chance of securing their election, especially if they took the Church's prohibitions against simony seriously.

That the episcopal office was a coveted one may be gauged from the disappointment and even anger some people felt when denied it. The rich and upwardly mobile also expected to secure the office when it fell vacant, regarding it as the pinnacle of their career. Candidates who came from families with a long history in the Church felt some sense of entitlement when an episcopal throne became available. We see this latter sense of keen disappointment in the case of the appointment of Epiphanius of Salamis, famous in history as the great fourth-century heresy hunter. Far from having a long history in the Church or impressive resources as a patron, he was a converted Jew and the son of a tenant farmer. When he became the bishop of Salamis, his clergy, resentful at being passed over in his favor, plotted to have him killed.

This strife and jockeying for the episcopal throne contrasts vividly with the earlier pre-Nicene process of election by the people (though even in the pre-Nicene period, people were still people and subject to the sin of ambition). Perhaps more than anything else, the degree to which the episcopal throne was coveted and regarded *by the public* as desirable witnesses to the magnitude of the Constantinian earthquake. In the third century, the local church was involved in choosing their bishop; now it was determined by his future episcopal peers. The bishop's throne, formerly a type of the throne of God,[32] now bore a striking resemblance to the throne of the emperor. Church authorities and writers had to insist again and again that the

---

32 The image of God on His throne and surrounded by His elders in Rev. 4:2–4 is clearly inspired by the image of the bishop and his presbyters on their throne.

episcopate was a work, not an honor, precisely because now it *was* popularly regarded as an honor.

The Church's recognition that worldly ambition for the bishop's throne needed to be curbed is perhaps behind the new insistence on ordaining a bishop only after he had already passed through the previous ranks of "lesser" clergy. We have seen that in the pre-Nicene Church with its organic understanding of church life, each clerical rank was valued for itself, not regarded as a further step on a hierarchical ladder. In those days, ordinations could proceed with a baptized candidate for the episcopate being ordained as bishop immediately, without the necessity of being made reader, deacon, and presbyter. With the advent of a more hierarchical understanding of church office, these kind of ordinations ceased, and episcopal candidates did indeed have to receive previous ordinations through the various ranks.

We see here how that hierarchical understanding of ordination could also possess a more pastoral function. The mere careerist candidate, one with no prior experience in the Church, expected to enter into episcopal office and honor at once. By insisting that candidates should have passed through the ranks of deacon and presbyter, the Church pushed back against such careerism and asserted that the leaders of the Church should have ecclesiastical experience. For this reason, the second canon of the Council of Nicea decreed that a man ordained to the episcopate "not be a neophyte," and canon 10 of the Council of Sardica a few years later decreed the same thing, for it was "not fitting . . . to proceed to this act rashly or lightly." The desire of the people for a patron and worldly connections of the secular candidate sometimes meant the canon was followed in letter rather than in spirit, as "neophytes" were rushed through the "lesser orders" on consecutive days. This practice of following the letter of the canon while violating its spirit shows how much pressure the Church felt itself under from the times in which it lived.

In short, the bishop as patron of his city was increasingly drawn into the network (some would say "the web") of the public life of the empire. The bishops moved in the upper echelons of society, rubbing shoulders with provincial governors and men of privilege, and so the state had an increased interest in what sort of men the bishops were. That accounts for the increased control the state tried to exercise over the Church's episcopate. In Constantine's day, there were no civic laws relating to offenses for which bishops could be disciplined or deposed. Those matters were left to the Church. By the days of Justinian, laws were passed determining for which offenses a bishop might be suspended (playing at dice and attending the games), and for which offenses he might be deposed (violating tombs and simony). As a public figure, the bishop was now accountable to the state as well as the Church.

The Bishop as Monk

Wealthy men were not the only candidates popular with the people. Synesius might have been the preferred candidate for the see of Ptolemais despite his Neoplatonism and his lack of spiritual gifts, but there were others who were preferred precisely because of their possession of such gifts. These were the holy men, men who were regarded as having walked with God and who knew Him intimately. The figure of the ascetic holy man, well known in the late antique Roman world, was also often desired as the people's choice, and a number of episcopal positions were filled by monks in the fourth century. This fact does not contradict the notion that the people chose men for their bishops who could function as their patrons, for there were many ways this patronage could be exercised.

Ascetical qualifications for clergy had always been a part of the Church's tradition, even from the days of St. Paul. In his First Epistle to Timothy and his Epistle to Titus, he insists that those chosen to be leaders in the Church be "above reproach, the husband of one wife, temperate, prudent, respectable, hospitable, able to teach, not addicted to wine, or a striker, but gentle, uncontentious, free from the love of money" (1 Tim. 3:2–3), "not self-willed, not quick-tempered, not fond of sordid gain, but good, sensible, just, devout, self-controlled" (Titus 1:7–8). At this early stage, the apostolic emphasis stressed stability and respectability, not extraordinary ascetic holiness. But in the first generation of new converts, the fruit of extraordinary ascetic holiness was perhaps harder to find. The seed that would blossom into St. Antony the Great had just been planted.

Further, the Church's appreciation of personal asceticism was not unique to her. In pagan thought also, it was believed that a true and reliable philosophy ought to include some ascetic rigor and disciplined chastity. Even Emperor Julian aspired to some rigorous abstemiousness in his personal pursuit of the philosophical life. The Church therefore could hardly ignore this ideal and the prestige that came from it if it was not only to please God, but to win the hearts of the people and convert them. The bishop was traditionally a man of holiness and devotion.

Asceticism had thus always been esteemed in the pre-Nicene Church. In the West, this esteem found eventual expression from the days of Pope Siricius (384–399) in the attempt to impose sexual continence on deacons, presbyters, and bishops. This discipline was not followed in the East, which continued to allowed clergy to cohabit with their wives and enjoy what it called the "use of marriage," possibly because the East had an eye on sectarian groups that had a more gnostic view of marriage. But even in the East the bishops were encouraged to maintain continence, especially in large cities, and in the fourth century many bishops were already celibate. No doubt the esteem accorded to monastics had something to do with this. Also, part of the bishop's task was to consecrate virgins,[33] and

---

33 Note the sneer of Jerome (in Epistle 69) at newly appointed bishops with no previous church experience: "Recently a fan of actors, now a consecrator of holy virgins!"

it was thought odd that the consecrator of virgins should not be celibate himself. Further, since the bishop controlled great wealth, it was thought prudent to elect to the office single men who had no families to support and who would be less tempted to mix ecclesiastical wealth with their own.

Yet though the Church always had a tradition of consecrated continence, monasticism was new. It began small in Egypt, Syria, and Palestine, and continued to grow. Its roots go far back. When Antony left the world for a life of asceticism, he was not the first one to make such a renunciation. Even in his day, there were groups of "renunciants" who lived on their own land in a state of ascetic isolation, celibacy, and prayer. Antony's novelty was not in his embrace of the ascetic life, but in his distance from settled communities.

Once the monastic movement embodied by Antony began, it grew unevenly and took different forms in different places. In Egypt, with its well-defined topography of city and desert, the monastic movement took the form of formal withdrawal from the settled city. This withdrawal did not, as previously imagined, involve the monks moving to great distances. And of course the Pachomian cenobitic monastery of the communal type was a kind of community unto itself, transplanted near the communities of "the world," and in fact the monastery of Pachomius was simply called "the Village."[34]

---

[34] Andrea Sterk, *Renouncing the World Yet Leading the Church* (Cambridge: Harvard University Press, 2004), p. 13. Her work here is the source for much of this present section.

In Syria, early asceticism took the form of "single ones" pledging themselves to celibacy, sometimes when they were baptized, and living at home or in small groups within the local church community. In Asia Minor, with its harsher winters, retreat into the wilderness was impractical. Accordingly, the ascetics practiced their asceticism within the city. The varieties of monasticism prove its popularity, for it was embraced by people throughout the empire in a variety of climates and locales. And the flexibility of the new movement helped to contribute to its popularity. One could become a monk regardless of where one lived. The movement held a fascination for many.

Yet throughout the fourth century, appreciation of ascetic holiness did not immediately produce instant and universal acceptance of the new monastic movement. In the pre-Nicene Church, personal asceticism was considered to be part of the normal Christian life, and such a life was lived as part of the church—that is, in the local church, in the city, centered around its bishop. Christianity was essentially an urban phenomenon, and so asceticism was considered to be an urban practice too. The ascetics of Egypt labored at their asceticism within the towns and villages, on the fringes of properties perhaps, but not distant from them.

The Eucharist, and therefore the parish, was the matrix in which Christian life was lived and sanctity pursued. It was because of this that when some men fled from this life and pursued sanctity apart from it, the bishops were initially alarmed.

Had not the Lord said that His Church was to be *in* the world, though not *of* it? What were they to make of men who somehow ignored this and chose no longer to be in the world? Gregory of Nazianzus lamented that monks were often the object of scorn, but even he was forced to acknowledge that the monks of his native Nazianzus were "the overzealous part of the church."[35] The council of Chalcedon in the fifth century would find it necessary to remind the monks that they were canonically subject to their local bishop.[36]

We can gauge the level of this suspicion and hostility by the tone of the works written to defend the new ascetic trends. John Chrysostom, for example, felt obliged to rush to the passionate defense of virgins and monks with all his customary zeal. In his book *On Virginity*, written perhaps in 381, he defends women who have embraced virginity and who refused to marry. This asceticism was usually pursued by women from within the safety and confines of the city, given the dangers to women living alone in the desert or the wilderness; but it nonetheless represented a genuine asceticism, one that was increasingly popular in the fourth century. But this ascetical impulse still flew in the face of many who regarded civic duties and obligations to be paramount, including the duty of having children.

It would be wrong to read this treatise as John's final word about sexuality and marriage, or indeed as if this were his

---

35 Oration 18, cited by Sterk, *op. cit.*, p. 33.
36 Canon 4: "In each city and country area, let the monks be subject to the bishop."

focus at all. John is not here calmly writing a theology of sexuality, striving to find balance. He writes as a knight, rushing to defend the embattled and belittled women who had chosen the good part (compare Luke 10:42) and were suffering for it. But the point is that there were plenty of people attacking those who had chosen this path.

It is the same with Chrysostom's work *Against the Enemies of Monasticism*. The fact that it was written in three volumes testifies to the importance John gave it. He defends the monks inhabiting the hills near Antioch. People within the city had not only disdained and criticized the monks, but had even been violent against them, beating them up and then boasting about it in town. Those inflicting the violence were "upper-class citizens who were getting fed up with the success the monks were having in recruiting their teenage sons to the harsh life of their settlements."[37] This shows not only the initial opposition of some within the Church to the new movement, but also the movement's increasing popularity, especially with the young. Monasticism was the wave of the future, and some of the solid and traditional Christians of Antioch were not happy about it.

Sometimes monastic excesses gave people reason for unhappiness. The Council of Gangra, meeting perhaps around 341, reacted to a group or movement associated with the ascetic Eustathius. Whether or not Eustathius was personally guilty

---

37 J.N.D. Kelly, *Golden Mouth* (Ithaca: Cornell University Press, 1995), p. 45.

of all the excesses denounced in the canons is an open question, but certainly the movement that swirled about him contained excessive elements.

Yet despite these growing pains, monasticism grew and commended itself to more and more of the people. By the end of the fourth century, the innovative monastic movement was becoming assimilated to the mainstream Church, and people increasingly viewed monks with favor. That is, while the rank and file appreciated the wealth of the upper-class bishop and his ability to function as their patron and helper, they looked to the monastic bishop with a different sort of esteem. The former might prevail with the state; the latter could prevail with God. The Church therefore often chose bishops who had been monks. Athanasius was keen to appoint many monks to bishoprics in his Egyptian sphere of influence, citing the pressing need of his day to find episcopal candidates who were both orthodox (i.e., pro-Nicea) and of blameless character. The preference for celibacy in the episcopate rapidly translated into a preference for the monasticism of the episcopate.

Overview of the Episcopate in the Fourth Century

The bonds uniting the layman with his bishop were stretched and transformed in the fourth century. Prior to this time, the layman felt himself united to his bishop by virtue of the closeness of their connection and by what they shared in common. The bishop's relation to the laity was the close relation of shepherd to flock. He knew them by name (compare John 10:3–4) and was intimately involved in their lives through his sacramental ministrations. They shared much in common—a small, intimate, and frequently endangered community, and the possibility of martyrdom. The author of the Book of Revelation wrote to his flock in Asia Minor as one who was their "brother, and fellow partaker in the tribulation and kingdom and perseverance which are in Jesus" (Rev. 1:9), and this description aptly summed up what was shared by the bishop and his flock throughout the pre-Nicene period. In short, the laity appreciated their bishop because of his closeness to them.

This was transformed in the fourth century. The bishop, whether a member of the landowning class and a man about town or a monk fulfilling a new urban calling, now related to his flock in terms of distance. If the bishop was chosen because of his social position and wealth, he was of use to the people because he was wealthier than they were and occupied a higher and more influential place. If chosen because of his monastic holiness, he was of use because he lived on a higher spiritual plane. In both cases, it was the *distance* of the bishop from his flock that defined and constituted his value to them.

Formerly, the flock looked to the bishop as a *pastor* who shared their lot (and who could therefore help them). Now they looked to a *patron* who did *not* share their lot (and who could therefore help them). If the fourth-century patron shared their lot of poverty, political powerlessness, or poor prayer life, he could be of little use to his flock. That is why the laity took care to choose men different from themselves, men who lived, either economically or spiritually, on a higher level. The help the episcopal patron afforded no doubt was much appreciated by the laity who received it. But it meant they felt less day-to-day connection with their bishop than formerly.

Instead, that day-to-day connection of laity with clergy was transferred to the presbyters. This acted to separate even further the formerly close connection of bishop with presbyter. Throughout the fourth century, the bishop thought of himself less and less as a fellow-presbyter (as in 1 Pet. 5:1) and more as the ruler over the presbyters. We must not of course exaggerate. The bishop had been transformed from pastor to patron, but he was still the patron of the city in which his people lived. He still maintained a geographical proximity to them and could be seen by them in the city. This would later change. But in the fourth century, the fact that the bishop and the people shared life in the same city meant the bonds joining shepherd and flock had not been entirely severed, merely changed.

The success the fourth-century episcopate had in meeting the challenges of their time was good for the Church's project of Christianizing society. But in its interior life, it eroded and destroyed what was left of the organic conception of Church as body. In looking up to the bishop as to someone higher than themselves (either economically or spiritually), the laity lost some of the awareness of their own ecclesial status, sanctity, and importance for the functioning of the Church. We see this especially in the increasing popularity of celibates or monks as bishops. The people esteemed the monastic bishop for his spirituality and looked up to him as to a person of superior holiness. This had the effect of equating holiness with monasticism and of furthering the equation of "lay" with "profane."

In the pre-Nicene Church, total commitment to God was expressed through baptism, and one left "the world" by becoming a Christian. The baptized Christian was "a stranger and an exile on the earth" (1 Pet. 2:11). With the celibate or monastic bishop as the increasing norm, one now expressed one's total commitment to God through becoming a monk. The eschatological dimension of the non-monastic Christian life had been lost. Monks were now the ones with the spiritual gifts. A "lay spiritual gift" (or non-monastic spiritual gift) was seen as a contradiction in terms. The dignity of the laity continued to sink ever lower. This monasticization of spirituality would continue in the centuries to come. It will be examined further below.

CHAPTER

FIVE

THE BISHOP IN BYZANTIUM & BEYOND
The Imperial Monk

FROM HIS EARLY ROOTS in the renunciants of Egypt and the "single ones" of Syria, the figure of the monk continued to grow until it dominated the Church. It was not as if the monks forced themselves on the Church. On the contrary, the faithful saw in the monks a dedication and heroism that inspired them. The laity freely followed the monks' lead, imitated their approach, and embraced their spirituality. The increasing popular expectation that bishops would be celibate quickly became the expectation that they would be monastic, and after this, popular expectation became an official and even imperial demand.

The Monasticization of the Episcopate

This process accelerated with the reign and legislation of Justinian (reigned 527–565). Justinian, as we have seen, took a great personal interest in the office and behavior of bishops. Under his rule, the selection of bishops was strictly controlled, and married men were no longer eligible for promotion to the episcopate. Indeed, those men who had been married but were now widowed were still barred from promotion if they had living children—doubtless because of the perceived temptation to appropriate church funds for support of family. The Church at the time did not protest this ruling but accepted such imperial laws as binding. The Church and state worked very closely together, and it was sometimes difficult to tell where one left off and the other began.

In 692, the Church passed a collection of canons referred to later as "the council *in Trullo*," so named because it was held in the hall under the dome (in Greek, *troulos*) where the Sixth Ecumenical Council had been held in Constantinople. As neither the Fifth nor Sixth Ecumenical Council had issued any canons, the council in Trullo is sometimes called the fifth–sixth council or the Quinisext council. One of the canons in this collection sets the seal on these prior developments. It is interesting to note that the relevant canon makes no reference to the previous imperial legislation. That is doubtless because the bishops considered themselves as responding to the divine law of God, not the changeable laws of the emperor. One would never guess from reading the canon that the matter had effectively been decided by Justinian over a century before. These imperial laws are simply taken for granted.

A part of the relevant canon 12 reads, "This has come to our knowledge, that in Africa and Libya and in other places the most God-beloved bishops in those parts do not refuse to live with wives, even after ordination, thereby giving scandal and offense to the people. Since therefore it is our particular care that all things tend to the good of the flock, it has seemed good that henceforth nothing of the kind shall in any way occur." The canon goes on to acknowledge that a married episcopate had previously been allowed by earlier canons (thought by them to be apostolic), but that now this change must be made in order "to give no offense, neither to the Jews, nor to the Greeks, nor to the church of God" (quoting Paul in 1 Cor. 10:32).

The rationale for the canon is that the Church should not give offense or cause for scandal, and a married episcopate in some parts of the world was causing just that. Rome and the West had for some time restricted its clergy to the unmarried, as canon 13 of the same Quinisext collection acknowledges. Western practice required that even those to be ordained a deacon or presbyter promise to cease from the use of marriage with their wives. This being the case, one can understand that a bishop refusing to cease cohabiting with his wife would cause scandal in the West. And as noted above, Emperor Justinian had closed that possibility in the East also. For this reason the canon says candidates for the episcopate are required to (or, more accurately, reminded to) abstain from cohabiting with their wives, if already married.

Note that this canon 12 does not require that the bishops be monastic or even have monastic experience. It assumes some bishops ordained are already married and demands simply that marital cohabitation cease forthwith. The issue here was not the glory of monasticism or the opportunities for holiness monasticism presented. The issue was sex. What was required was the physical celibacy of the bishop, not his involvement in monasticism.

What should the wife of the newly ordained bishop do? Canon 48 of the Trullan council decreed that she and her now-episcopal husband separate by mutual consent and she go and live in a women's monastery, stipulated as "situated at a distance from the abode of the bishop." (It appears that the council Fathers wanted to ensure that no "visiting" went on between former husband and wife.) The former wife was to be provided for by her husband-bishop. She could become a deaconess (by then a strictly honorary position) "if she is deemed worthy." How many women in that situation availed themselves of the proffered sop is not known. One senses some slight embarrassment on the part of the council Fathers in mandating what was essentially a divorce.

Though the Trullan council's canons do not mandate a monastic episcopate or that non-monastic candidates for the episcopate become monks, this canon could not but further the perception in the popular mind that a bishop should be a monk—especially since for many years bishops were expected to be single. Thus, in the years following the Trullan council, though the canonical requirement had not changed to demand that bishops be monks, the expectation that bishops be monastic increased. By the eighth century, the hagiographical tradition was largely silent about married bishops. If bishops were required to be celibate, the monastery was the obvious place to look for bishops. No further canonical demand was required for the episcopate to become monastic. Monasteries became breeding grounds for bishops.

Though monasticism continued to grow in popular esteem, it was not until after the Church's triumph over iconoclasm that the monks finally secured their place at the episcopal helm of the Church. After the long struggle against iconoclasm ended with the victory of icons as championed by the monks, a monastic grip on the episcopate was assured. The monks had suffered and shed their blood in defense of the truth, and this heroic sacrifice gave them an almost invincible moral authority. From the ninth century onward, bishops would be monks.

The rise of hesychasm in the fourteenth century and the triumph over his detractors of Gregory Palamas (canonized a mere nine years after his repose—a sure sign of his popularity and the ascendancy of his hesychastic theology) would exalt the monastic ideals even further and confirm the equation of spirituality with monasticism. Gregory's theology began with a defense of the view that monks, through their asceticism and the grace of God it could bring, could actually see the uncreated light of divinity. The holy man of the fourth century was revered as one who could see God in the sense of knowing Him through his great purity of heart: "Blessed are the pure of heart, for they shall see God" (Matt. 5:8). The holy man could see God with the enlightened and purified eyes of his heart. But here was a claim to see the uncreated light of divinity with the physical eyes of the body. In this vision, only the monk was fit to lead.

This monasticization of the episcopate brought with it also a similar monasticization of spirituality in general. As the Christian Faith spread and took root and leavened the lump of the empire more and more, the dividing line separating the world and the Kingdom became harder to find, as witnessed in the popular desire to secure as bishops men who were rich and successful in the world. This meant the eschatological focus of the monks became all the more attractive and all the more important.

In the pre-Nicene period, total commitment to Christ was expressed in baptism, for all the baptized risked martyrdom to a greater or lesser extent. Now baptism brought no such risk, but on the contrary, the promise of social advancement. How then could one express total commitment to Christ? Many chose monasticism as the expression of this commitment. Thus, the further from monasticism one was, the further from holiness. The only real spirituality available to the Christian was to be found in a monastery. Everything else was at best a second-rate substitute.

This conviction is found in the monastic literature itself, in its grudging concession that non-monastics also may be saved. Take for example the classic *Ladder of Divine Ascent*, written by John, the abbot of the monastery in Mount Sinai, in about 600—a book written by a monk and for monks. In its very first chapter, on renunciation of life, we read:

> Someone caught up in the affairs of the world can make progress, if he is determined. But it is not easy. Those bearing chains can still walk. But they often stumble and are thereby injured. The man who is unmarried and in the world, for all that he may be burdened, can nevertheless make haste toward the monastic life. But the married man is like someone chained hand and foot. Some people living carelessly in the world put a question to me, "How can we who are married and living amid public cares aspire to the monastic life?" I answered: "Do whatever good you may. Speak evil of no one. Rob no one. Tell no lie.... If you do all this, you will not be far from the kingdom of heaven."[38]

This passage is revealing for the assumptions it makes. The non-monastics (the overwhelming part of the Church) are described not merely as "living in the world," but as "caught up in the affairs of the world." The author acknowledges that such

---
38 *Ladder of Divine Ascent*, Step 1.

a person "can make progress," but the amount of progress will depend upon how closely he can approximate "the monastic life"—here equated with progress and spirituality. If one in the world is single and celibate, he is still chained (by virtue of not being monastic). But he can still "walk" and make haste toward holiness. But one living in the world and married is "like one chained hand and foot"—not able to make progress at all, much less make haste.

When the question is pressed whether it is possible for such a married person to aspire to salvation (again equated with "the monastic life"), the answer is given that if such a person does his best to live a virtuous life, he "will not be far from the kingdom of heaven." This is not a ringing endorsement of his salvation, especially when one realizes that the phrase "not far from the kingdom of heaven" was used by Christ to describe a Jewish scribe *who was not yet a Christian* (Mark 12:34). For John Climacus, monasticism is all but equated with Christianity. The married in the world may be saved, but by the skin of their non-monastic teeth. This represents a complete revolution from the thought of the pre-Nicene Church, which gave no inkling that holiness was impossible for those in the world who remained married.

The Sacralization of Power

In the Roman Empire, the emperor was considered a sacred figure. The divine dignity of the emperor in pagan times gave way to a revision of this imperial dignity in Christian times, but even in this reconfiguration, the emperor lost little of his aura. He was now the Lord's anointed, one who functioned as a secular kind of bishop over the world, even as church leaders were bishops over the Church. By virtue of being God's instrument in the world, he was *isapostolos,* equal to the apostles. It was a commonplace in Orthodox canon law that the emperor "represented" the laity in church decisions, taking their place and supplying their voice.[39] In the Byzantine symphony of Church and state working together, the emperor balanced the power of the Church.

Not surprisingly, therefore, as the empire with its twin powers of Church and state collapsed, the power of the Church alone was left standing. The sacred aura surrounding the emperor fell then to the bishops. As the empire weakened and finally collapsed in 1453, the demise of the emperor left a vacuum. In terms of political power, it was not possible of course for the bishops to fill the vacuum, since the armies of Islam and their ruler now sat on the imperial throne. The episcopate after 1453 became "monarchical" in the truest sense of the term. Previously the power of the bishop had been counterbalanced by the laity and the presbyters (in the pre-Nicene

---

39 Discussion of the following details may be found in Vassa Larin, *The Byzantine Hierarchal Divine Liturgy in Arsenij Suxanov's Proskinitarij* (Rome: Pontificio Istituto Orientale, 2010) and in her "The Hierarchal Liturgy in Late Byzantium and After" in SVS Quarterly, vol. 55, number 1.

Church), or the imperial power (in Byzantium), but no longer.

This was especially true in Russia in the late sixteenth century. The development was facilitated by the tremendous sizes of the episcopal dioceses there, which gave to the bishops an aura of even greater power—as did the fact that they were scarcely seen by the local parishes. Their visits resembled those of a potentate, and the liturgical details of the pontifical rituals served to reinforce this. Episcopal power had fused with political power, and church rituals celebrated this fusion. This celebration and sacralization of power is apparent when we examine the details and evolution of the episcopal ritual.

First we note the growing differentiation between the presbyteral and the episcopal liturgies during this period and an increased solemnification of the latter. Originally there were few distinctions between the ways a bishop and presbyter served, but differences tended to multiply as time went by. We note the use of a two-handed blessing of the people by the bishop after the mid-seventeenth century, for which there was no previous precedent. Prior to this time, the bishop blessed the people with one hand, as did his presbyters.

Another development representing the "episcopization" of the ritual is the solemn vesting rite for bishops, which previously did not differ from the vesting rite for presbyters. The ritual for the vesting prayers gives biblical verses to be recited while each vestment is put on, which do not appear in Byzantine euchologies until the twelfth and thirteenth centuries. Originally this devotional verse was phrased in the first person singular (e.g., the prayer for putting on the belt: "Blessed is God who girds *me* with strength"). In the pontifical changes, the bishop vests while the deacon chants the biblical verses, changing the first person singular to the second person singular (e.g., "Blessed is God who girds *you* with strength"). The bishop originally vested privately in the narthex or before entering the church. The vesting was done and the verses were said in private, for the celebrant's benefit alone. In the new ritual, he enters the nave and is vested by others in the center while others chant aloud the prescribed verses and cense him. Clearly the vesting and verses were now done for the benefit of others, as part of the glorification of the bishop's office.

Yet another difference between the original and transformed rituals is the greater use of the episcopal *omophorion*. Originally the omophorion was a kind of scarf, its use limited to the processional moment of the bishop's entrance and emblematic of his episcopal rank. Once the bishop entered the altar and sat on his throne at the High Place in the apse, he removed it for the readings. The omophorion was not necessary for the ensuing sacramental celebration, which he served without it, just as presbyters did. The omophorion was a vestment of honor; the right to wear it was not shared by all bishops.

The council of Constantinople IV in 869–870 tried to regulate its use. Canon 27 (14) of that council decreed, "Bishops who have been permitted to wear the omophorion at certain times must not abuse so great and honorable a garment through pride, vainglory, human conceit, and self-love, by wearing it unnecessarily throughout the Divine Sacrifice." This canonical legislation could not withstand the rising tide of sacralization, and the omophorion was indeed used after the episcopal entrance during the ensuing sacramental celebration.

Yet another detail involved the increased use of "eagle rugs," the small circular rug with an eagle pictured on it upon which the bishop stands. Originally, in the fourteenth century, when bishops were ordained, an eagle was drawn with chalk on the floor, and the episcopal candidate stood upon it when he was ordained. This practice was changed so that the Russians inheriting the practice of drawing an eagle on the floor now produced a portable embroidered eagle rug. The Greeks only used such rugs at episcopal ordinations, but the Russians used them extensively throughout the service.

Another detail relates to the episcopal *mantiya*, or cloak. Monastics wore such cloaks as a sign of their monastic state, in simple unadorned black. With the increased grandeur of the bishop's office, this piece of clothing was adorned with long, multicolored stripes, said to depict the teaching that flows from the mouth of the bishop. Eventually, in the sixteenth and seventeenth centuries, the *mantiya* of the patriarch was further adorned to appear distinct from the *mantiyas* of other bishops.

We note next a number of appropriations of imperial ritual by the bishop. First is the acclamation *"Eis polla eti despota,"*

"Many years, Master!" This was not found in any Greek pontifical before the fourteenth or fifteenth century. It had its origins in the popular acclamations of the emperor at imperial processions and civil festivals. In the earlier form of the episcopal acclamation used in the early fourteenth century, the bishop is hailed with "Many years, Father!" but this later changes to the episcopized form "Master."

We next note the *sakkos*, the embroidered tunic worn by bishops. It was originally an honorific vestment worn by Roman consuls and later by the Byzantine emperor. The privilege of wearing it was given to the patriarch of the imperial city of Constantinople as a special honor sometime in the eleventh century. The wearing of the sakkos by other patriarchs and even some distinguished archbishops followed, and Symeon of Thessalonica in the early fifteenth century writes that it was worn by "the more eminent of the bishops" in his day. In the fifteenth century in Russia, it was worn by the metropolitan of Moscow but not by other Russian bishops. Under the reign of Peter the Great (1621–1725), all Russian bishops began to wear the sakkos.

Finally we note the wearing of the episcopal miter or crown. Perhaps nothing else suggests and visually embodies the imperial role of the bishop like his crown. The Greek miter now worn by all Orthodox bishops was introduced into the Russian church by Patriarch Nikon in 1653. The wearing of the miter was originally a privilege given to the patriarch of

Constantinople and extended to all bishops after the fall of the city in 1453. Indeed, Symeon of Thessalonica writes in the early part of that century that although the patriarch of Alexandria and many others wore miters, "the more binding" custom was for bishops to serve bareheaded.

In surveying all these liturgical usages and vestment customs, we observe a consistent and increasing tendency to aggrandize the office and person of the bishop, differentiating him from his presbyters and bestowing upon him an imperial bearing. It is the combination of the imperial appropriations by the bishop that contributes to his sacralization. In the fourth century, the bishop changed from being a local pastor to a local patron. He now changes still further from being a patron to a person of power. With the sacralization of this power, the bishop effectively places himself beyond the reach of any earthly accountability.

Overview of the Byzantine Episcopate

By the end of the post-Byzantine period we have surveyed above, the office and role of the bishop have changed out of all recognition from that of the pre-Nicene period. It is still the bishop who was responsible for ordinations, and his Eucharist was still "constitutionally" the main one of his (now far-flung) diocese, but everything else has changed. We may list three of these radical changes, most of which still remain in the office of bishop in Orthodoxy today.

Firstly, the bishop was no longer the main pastor for the people in his diocesan flock. That role was now filled by the presbyteral parish priest. The bishop no longer exercised any real pastoral function for the majority of his flock. His was not the hand that fed them with the Eucharist, nor the hand that baptized them, nor the hand that married them, nor the hand that buried their dead.

Secondly, the bishop's presbyters no longer exercised any check on his power and had no consultative function. Instead, they were entirely within his power and served at his pleasure. The parishes remained entirely passive under his authority.

Finally, the bishop's diocese now was often large and sometimes vast, so that he usually no longer saw all his diocesan flock. Sometimes the rank and file saw their bishop infrequently; some saw him almost never. If and when he did visit, he was often accompanied by his retinue, and the visit resembled that of a head of state or foreign potentate.

The far-reaching effects of each of these three points could be elaborated at some length. Suffice it to say that little remained of the original structural arrangements set up by the apostles that prevailed throughout the pre-Nicene period.

In the Byzantine and post-Byzantine periods, the bishop is distant from his presbyters and even more distant from his people. There is little opportunity for them to get to know him or thus to love him. The bishop in turn must seek his support and friendships elsewhere, in the company of monastics, his retinue, friends in high places, or fellow bishops. The close relationship of fellowship between bishop, presbyters, and diocese/local church that characterized life in the early Church has effectively broken down.

The presbyters serve at a distance from each other and do not share their pastoral load as a team, which adds to the strain of their pastoral office. Accordingly, they labor in degrees of emotional isolation from one another, find themselves completely dependent upon their parish, and feel themselves unsupported when tensions arise between parish and priest.

The people relate to their parish priest sacramentally but need have no intimate relationships with each other that are rooted in church membership. Obviously members of the same village will know one another, and members of the same parish may get to know one another. But these relationships are rooted in the dynamics of village or voluntary grouping, and determined by individual personality and decision. They are not, as in the pre-Nicene Church, rooted in mutual membership in the local body of Christ.

Accordingly, one sees individualism enshrined at the center of piety. For example, one now receives the Eucharist for one's own private spiritual benefit and as the expression of one's personal piety—not (as before) as the corporate and self-defining act of the local church. Gathering around the bishop and his presbyters for the Sunday Eucharist was the spiritual and sacramental glue that held the people together. In the post-Byzantine world, the bishop is now far away, and his presbyters scattered, serving throughout the often vast diocese. The relational unity of the local church has broken down, to be replaced with the legal and bureaucratic unity of scattered parishes being served by the same distant church administrator.

CHAPTER

THE BISHOP IN THE NEW WORLD
The Important Visitor

IN THE TWENTIETH CENTURY, the world experienced tremendous upheavals, such as the Russian Revolution, the spread of communism, and two world wars, and the Orthodox Church was profoundly affected by all of it. As possibilities for transportation grew, the world also became a much smaller place (eventually Marshall McLuhan would coin the term "global village"), and immigration and the shifting of populations continued on an increasing scale. This meant the Orthodox Church of the East eventually found itself in the West as well, as the terms "Western Church" and "Eastern Church" came to describe not so much those churches' geography as their historical lineage.

The Eastern Orthodox Church Goes West

By the term "West," one can mean many things beyond simple geographical facts. Both Australia and the United States are considered as parts of "the West," since the term can be used culturally as well as geographically, and indeed the Orthodox churches in both Australia (for example) and the United States share many similarities. Here, however, we will focus our attention mostly upon the Church in North America, since America is the cultural epicenter of the West, and also because the Church here is better known to the present author.

The presence of the Orthodox Church in North America is the result of both mission and immigration. In 1793, a group of Russian missionaries left the western parts of Russia to travel eastward across the continent on the way to Russian Alaska in order to missionize the Native Americans there. They arrived in Alaska in 1794. This group was self-consciously missionary; they came not simply as chaplains to the Russians of the Russian American Trading Company of enterprising fur traders, which was then working in Alaska, but also and mostly to evangelize the non-Christian native peoples there. Foremost among the group was the monk Herman, later canonized in 1970 as St. Herman of Alaska.

This original group of missionaries was followed by others, such as Fr. John Veniaminov (later canonized as St. Innocent), who arrived with his family in 1824 to build upon the original foundations. From these beginnings, the Russian Church established an American missionary diocese under (now Bishop) Innocent. Bishop Innocent was a gifted and visionary worker who suggested Orthodoxy should do missionary work in the United States. To this end, he suggested to his synod that the services and liturgical books for his diocese be translated into English; that American-born men be sought out as quickly as possible as candidates for the priesthood; and that an English-speaking bishop be immediately installed. Eventually the Russian diocese expanded into the western parts of the "lower forty-eight." The see came to be established in San Francisco.

This original missionary diocese received an unexpected boost in numbers through the work of Fr. Alexis Toth, who was working in the eastern United States as an Eastern-rite Catholic priest from 1889. His frustrations with his unsupportive local Western-rite Roman Catholic bishop (under whose immediate supervision he was) led to his departure from Roman Catholicism and his reception into the Orthodox Church. Under Fr. Toth (later canonized as St. Alexis of Wilkes-Barre), many Eastern-rite Catholics became Orthodox. The original missionary diocese now had substantial numbers in both the western and eastern parts of the United States. Reflecting this mixed heritage, its official name (up until 1970) was "the Russian Orthodox Greek Catholic Church of America." During this time, its basic ethnic makeup was Russian and its liturgical language Slavonic.

Orthodoxy in North America also grew from successive waves of immigration, as more and more people from abroad came to the fabled Land of Liberty seeking a better life. Thus a number of Greeks, Russians, Serbs, Romanians, Ukrainians, Albanians, Bulgarians, and Lebanese came to Canada and the US, settling where they could. Some intended only to stay for a few years, make their fortunes, and return home, but others intended to settle down in their new land.

These new immigrants of course brought their faith with them, and quickly Orthodox churches sprang up in the New World. Each group struggled with the challenges faced by all new immigrants—learning a new language and finding work. They treasured and preserved their ancestral languages and customs, and found in their churches a vehicle not only to help them cope in their new environment but also to comfort them in preserving what was familiar from their old one. The new immigrants naturally clustered together, bringing clergy from "the old country" who would serve them in their separate ethnic enclaves. The already existing Russian missionary diocese provided some measure of unity and canonical covering for them, but each group tended to define itself by language and ethnicity, and so most groups simply went their own way. The immigration patterns were too haphazard to allow for interethnic canonical cohesion. The various ethnic groups of Orthodox in America never were fully administratively united.

As the Russian Revolution forced the original American

missionary diocese to face new challenges, its members became very conscious of their Russian heritage. The diocese also faced other challenges from rival Russian groups, as the original Russian American diocese splintered into various factions. During this time, the various ethnic groups of Orthodox in America also began to consolidate themselves into separate administrations, now called "jurisdictions." By 1930 many of them had organized themselves as exarchates, or dependencies of their Old World mother churches overseas. These jurisdictions of course overlapped one another geographically, but this did not affect the day-to-day life of the parishes, since they had become organized on ethnic and linguistic grounds, rather than on territorial ones. All this was very different from the situations of their mother churches overseas.

The Bishop in the New World: A Stranger in a Strange Land

These differences in the Orthodox Church's life in America compared to its life in its traditional countries could not but have a great impact on the bishops here as they strove to make sense of the American experience and to lead their flocks. These differences and the challenges they posed were many.

First of all was the tradition of pluralism in America, with its famous separation of church and state. It was almost axiomatic in Orthodox lands of origin that the state would support the Orthodox Church in the performance of her mission, including providing funding for clergy and for church projects—so much so that some have spoken of Orthodoxy after the breakup of Byzantium as "*Byzance après Byzance.*" The traditional troparion for the Feast of the Elevation of the Holy Cross prayed that God would grant victory to the Orthodox kings over the barbarians, but where in America were the Orthodox kings? (One Orthodox group would later amend the prayer to read, "grant victory to the Orthodox Christians over their adversaries.")

The American vision explicitly refused to establish a state Church or to privilege one denomination (as they were called) over another. The American government committed itself to a studied neutrality when it came to denominational quarrels. Pluralism was not merely a fact but a valued principle. One group might assume more importance than another, but such importance was based on the group's ability to lobby the government.

The Orthodox in America and Canada were comparatively few in number, scattered, and divided by language and culture. As such, they were in no position to do much effective lobbying, and the bishops found themselves as heads over small flocks, marginalized from the mainstream. This took some getting used to, for in their homelands a bishop was a socially significant figure by virtue of his being a leader in the state-favored Church—a significance which often involved a financial advantage as well. In North America, there was respect for religious leaders—any religious leaders—but simply being

Orthodox in itself brought no special preeminence, importance, or advantage.

Related to Orthodoxy's immigrant status in America was the fact of its apparent foreignness. All cultures are somewhat xenophobic and suspicious of foreigners, even if a large statue in the New York harbor does bid the world give America its tired, its poor, its huddled masses yearning to breathe free. America as a country was open and welcoming to immigrants, who saw it as a land of freedom and opportunity. That did not mean, however, that all its citizens were welcoming to foreigners. To be foreign was to be suspect and potentially second-class. That was why the immigrants strove to learn the American vernacular as quickly as they could and to fit in. They did not want to look or sound foreign but to be like others around them.

In this context, Orthodoxy looked very foreign indeed, and not simply because its services were conducted in foreign languages. It looked exotic, mysterious. The combination of foreign language, icons, incense, brocade vestments, and complicated rituals all combined to give an impression of something too foreign to be truly American. America had reached a stability and stasis when it came to Christianity or religion in general. Dogtags for American soldiers in the Second World War were stamped with "C" (for Catholic), "P" (for Protestant), or "H" (for Hebrew, or Jewish). Everyone knew Christians came in only two flavors, Protestant or Catholic. The presence of Orthodox Christians could only upset this stasis; no one quite knew at first where the Orthodox fit in. This did nothing to enhance the importance of the Orthodox Church nor that of its bishops.

Further, all of these factors—small numbers, relative cultural unimportance, apparent foreignness—provided reasons for Orthodox not only to strive for assimilation into the American mainstream, but sometimes even to leave the Orthodox Church for other, more socially acceptable ones. This move was aided by the fact that Orthodoxy had never taught, as Roman Catholicism did, that members of other churches were going to hell. Such generosity to the other denominations appeared to some Orthodox to make the other churches valid alternatives to Orthodoxy. Case in point: The Orthodox church enjoyed a warm relationship with the Anglican/Episcopal church, and some Orthodox found Anglicanism an acceptable alternative to Orthodoxy—not only when Orthodox churches were not available, but also sometimes when they were.

In response to this threat of potential loss, the Orthodox clergy stressed not so much the dogmatic superiority of Orthodoxy over its heterodox neighbors as loyalty to one's ethnic heritage: if one were a Russian (or a Greek or a Serb), then one should go to the Russian (or Greek or Serbian) Church. Temptations to leave the Orthodox Church were thus met by a renewed appreciation of and appeal to ethnic heritage. The result, of course, was that the Orthodox jurisdictions continued to define themselves by individual ethnic identity.

Also, because American Orthodoxy grew by immigration, there was little monastic presence here compared with the old countries of origin. Lay men and women might come to North America seeking a better life for themselves and their families. Bishops and parish priests might come here to serve their ethnic flocks in the American diaspora. But why would monastics come here? They were already well established in great numbers in their traditionally Orthodox homelands. A hermit from one of the monasteries might receive his abbot's blessing to move some distance and live in a small skete, as one of the monastery's dependencies. But even then he was still considered as part of that monastery. Why would any of the monks leave their monastery and their homeland to travel to America? Where would they settle here? And how? Would they even be welcome? The original mission to Alaska consisted entirely of monastics, but they came not so much to establish monasteries as to establish missions. For this reason there continued to be very few monasteries in North America compared to the number of monks back home. Laymen in the parishes who were accustomed to visiting the local monastery back home for spiritual support and direction found themselves in America without this important option.

A final difference between the church in the New World and the churches in the Old World lay in the bishops' inclusion in a wider synod or group of bishops. In the Old World, a bishop was part of a larger group more or less close by. He was subject to his patriarch or metropolitan and to his synod, and he could be supported by their fellowship. In the New World, these fellow bishops were far, far away. The bishop here found he must function day-to-day less as a member of a team and more as a missionary, if not an exile. In a word, serving in the diaspora could prove to be a difficult and lonely experience. Orthodox bishops serving their American flocks were indeed serving in a strange land.

Settling Down in the New World

Since most of the Orthodox immigrants came with plans to stay, the Orthodox Church in North America quickly outgrew its initial immigrant phase. It would still to a large extent be defined in terms of its various ethnicities, but it began to grow, mature, settle in, and assimilate culturally to its adopted land.

The new immigrants began to prosper in the succeeding generations, and their churches benefitted from this new prosperity. New and large church temples were built and adorned (and often filled with pews, as befitting proper American-style churches). Some jurisdictions founded and funded seminaries to train American-born men to be priests. Some monasteries began to be established, though this occurred only sporadically and on a much smaller scale than back in the homelands. Some jurisdictions began to use English for their liturgical services, partly because a number of their faithful had chosen marriage partners from outside their own ethnicity, and these non-Orthodox partners were more likely to attend Orthodox services if they were at least partly in English. As the churches grew and used more English, other converts came to Orthodoxy, drawn to the Church not by their choice of marriage partner, but out of genuine interest in the Orthodox Faith.

As Orthodox increased in numbers and strength in North America, the cause of inter-Orthodox and jurisdictional unity advanced as well. The desire for administrative unity among the jurisdictions for purposes of common action eventually led to the formation of the Standing Conference of Orthodox Bishops in America (SCOBA) in 1960. The various bishops continued to work together and concelebrate, helping their flocks to see that Orthodoxy was something more than mere ethnic custom. As well as working with other Orthodox, the Orthodox churches also took part in pan-Protestant and ecumenical organizations, such as the National Council of Churches—a definite sign of Orthodoxy's increased respectability and ecclesiastical importance in the American scene. The Orthodox churches were quickly coming of age in their adopted land, learning to fit into the new cultural landscape and to speak with a single and effective voice.

Recently at time of writing (in 2015), challenges have appeared on the horizon that could threaten Orthodoxy's continued cultural assimilation. As North America becomes more militantly secular and more openly opposed to the traditional teachings and values of Orthodoxy, particularly regarding issues of gender, sexuality, and abortion, the Orthodox churches in America will increasingly find themselves at odds with the prevailing secular culture. Orthodox Christians adhering to their traditional faith will fit into the North American mainstream less and less. Yet even here there are gains, since disagreements with the prevailing secular culture serve to underline for the Orthodox their inter-jurisdictional unity among themselves. Enforced cultural expulsion by the mainstream will help the different Orthodox ethnicities see afresh how much they have in common and how much they share as Orthodox, despite their different languages and cultures.

Overview of the Orthodox Episcopate in the New World

The process of effective separation of the bishop from his diocesan flock we saw in Byzantium escalated when the bishops moved to the New World. The bishops have little day-to-day connection with their flocks but visit each of their many parishes as time and energy allow. This separation is aided by the tremendous distances involved in serving in the North American continent. Compared to their ancestral homelands, Orthodox in North America are few in number and spread out.

The reduced numbers of laity in a bishop's diocese (compared to the situation in the Old World) is due to a number of factors. First of all, North American Orthodox are no longer organized on a *territorial* basis, and a diocese no longer consists of all the Orthodox living in a given city. Rather, Orthodoxy is organized on an *ethnic* basis, and a diocese consists of all the Orthodox of a *given ethnicity* living in a given area. That in itself makes for a smaller number of faithful under the bishop responsible for them. If Orthodox laity of all ethnic backgrounds in a certain locale were under his care, he would have a larger local flock there.

The smaller numbers of faithful are also the result of American pluralism. In Imperial Russia or Greece, one could assume most of the population was at least nominally Orthodox and had some connection to the Orthodox Church. This is not the case in North America. In America, most Christians in a given city are not Orthodox and have no connection with the Orthodox church or its bishop.

Organization according to ethnic principles rather than territorial ones means each of the bishops has to travel long distances to care for all the flock under his care, for the faithful are spread out and live in various cities and villages. This often involves a tremendous burden of travel for the bishop, and it is no surprise if he can do no more than pay an occasional visit to any one of his parishes. Despite his love and solicitude for the people, he is simply not able to be with them very often. He cannot function as their pastor but rather as a beloved and important visitor.

This necessary absence of the bishop from most of his parishes on any given Sunday means the effective acting head of the local parish is not the bishop, but the presbyter. Canonically he is there as the bishop's delegate, so that canonically it is the bishop who is the true head of the parish. Some[40] suggest that in fact the unity of the bishop's diocese has not been broken but merely stretched by its consisting of many parishes. Thus, despite how it may appear, there are not many Eucharists in the diocese, but simply an extension of the one episcopal Eucharist throughout time and space. Thus, the *synthronon* where the bishop traditionally sat with his presbyters has now been parceled out into different Eucharist centers. On this view, the diocese, whatever its size and geographical vastness, is still "the local church."

There are problems with this understanding of the local church and the parish. The unity of the church in the pre-Nicene days before the proliferation of presbyteral Eucharists was different. In that day, the unity the presbyters had with one another and with their bishop, and the unity of people with their bishop and with one another in the one "local church," were all tangible and experiential, rooted in what they experienced every Sunday. Their invariable experience involved seeing their bishop and all his presbyters every week. They came to church and saw each other, and were forged by their weekly experiences into a single community. Unity was an *experience*, not a legal concept. To imagine that the primordial pre-Nicene unity of *synthronon* remains intact today is to drive a

---

40 Such as Zizioulas.

wedge between legal concept and actual experience, between what canonists proclaim and what the people know from their experience to be true. The "local church" was "local" precisely because each person in it could see and serve every other in love. Being local had value only because it allowed for these loving possibilities. It seems clear that "the local church" is now the parish, not the diocese, and the functioning head of the local church is the parish priest, not the bishop.

This means all the clergy, including the bishop, serve in comparative isolation from one another. Orthodox clergy in the same diocese may (or may not) see each other regularly, but such contact is a far cry from the weekly intimate contact they experienced in the pre-Nicene Church, where they were aware of serving as part of the same team, and where they constantly saw, supported, and were supported by their bishop. The bishop now may but rarely see his clergy, however much he prays for them and cares for them.

This separation of bishop from his presbyters mirrors his separation (in most jurisdictions) from his brother bishops. If he is a member of a jurisdiction whose head is overseas, he will not often see the fellow members of his synod. Even in North America, given the division of Orthodoxy into separate jurisdictions, he may but rarely see his fellow bishops from the other jurisdictions. The clerical estate can be a lonely one for all concerned.

Further, the comparative dearth of monasticism in North

America means the bishop of a diocese will usually either have no effective monastic formation (if he is chosen from among the serving American clergy) or will come as a foreigner from overseas (if he does have monastic experience). Since about AD 692, the custom has been for bishops to be chosen from among the monks. But in North America there are few monks from which to choose the bishops, and such monasteries as exist here cannot provide the rich breeding ground for bishops that monasteries from overseas can, with their multiplicity of viable candidates. It is true that non-monastic episcopal candidates here can be found among the bachelor clergy, and these candidates can be tonsured as monks prior to episcopal consecration. But the rule of choosing monks as bishops had in mind something more than simple monastic tonsure. The rule presupposed that the monk bishop had the benefit of long experience of monastic training, formation, and holiness. Such experience is rarely available to episcopal candidates coming from North America. Here we must choose between having experienced monks or having local men.

Finally, the comparative marginalization of Orthodoxy and its lack of a privileged place in society (compared with its role in Byzantium) means that despite the bishop's impressive robes and impressive liturgy, he is a humble figure. Serving as bishop does not now guarantee access to the halls of worldly power nor any great amount of social prestige among the general population. This speaks well for the North American episcopate, for it means that there is less temptation to covet the office of bishop for unworthy reasons of worldly glory and career advancement. The bishop is likely to accept the office only out of a genuine desire to serve Christ and His Church. The gold of the bishop is now more likely to be found in his heart than in his pocket. One imagines the bishops of the pre-Nicene Church, as well as St. John Chrysostom, would be pleased.

PRACTICAL CONCLUSIONS
Filling the Empty Throne

HAVING EXAMINED AT LENGTH the history of the episcopate, we can see that our bishops in the West today are the inheritors of a long, complicated, and varied history. For all of its twists and turns and changes, the office of bishop is a glorious office, one instituted by Christ and resplendent with the light of martyrdom, for bishops from the earliest days until now have been in the forefront of those shedding their blood for the Master. They have stood both in the front lines of the Church's conflict with the world and also in the center of the Church's interior life. They have defined and preserved the Church's Faith as well as serving as the fountainhead of her sacramental grace. No wonder an old book describing the episcopate was entitled simply *The Apostolic Ministry*,[41] for there can be no apostolic church without its bishop.

The episcopate is a high and holy calling and one that requires courage. St. John Chrysostom warned of the magnitude of the difficulties facing bishops when he wrote, "When someone has to preside over the Church and be entrusted with the care of so many souls, then let all womankind give way before the magnitude of the task—and indeed most men."[42] Given such a challenging task, our first response to those who have taken on that burden must be one of gratitude. But the question remains: How can the Church at large help its bishops to fulfill their task most effectively? And what can we do to help at the local level?

The North American Church at large can help by consecrating more bishops and by multiplying the number of dioceses. If, for example, the North American Church were to double or even triple its number of bishops, that would create the opportunity for those bishops to care for dioceses that were half or even one-third the size they are now, so that bishops could visit their various parishes two or even three times more than they can at present. As we have seen, bishops were originally consecrated to be the heads of their communities, the voice each parishioner heard every Sunday and the face they looked upon when they received Holy Communion. The vast size of

---

41 Ed. K. E. Kirk (London: Hodder & Stoughton, 1946).
42 *On the Priesthood*, ch. 4.

episcopal dioceses means the bishops now can only rarely visit each parish. Smaller dioceses would make regular visitation of the parishes more possible.

The Church at large could also shift some of the burden of decision-making and administration from the bishop to his presbyters. Possibly the bishop might create (or rather restore) a council of presbyters in his diocese to assist him in his work. Not all the presbyters of a diocese need serve in this way at the same time; possibly membership in the bishop's council might involve a revolving rota, with each of the diocesan presbyters taking their turn. Such an offloading of administrative responsibility would free up the bishop to be the pastor and teacher he was called to be.

And what can we do as members of local congregations? Here we need to strengthen the bonds between bishop and parishioner and take steps to make sure they are the bonds of love.

Firstly and most importantly, we should invite the bishop to come as often as he can, so that he is experienced as a pastor, friend, and father. Now he is present mostly as an important visitor; we need him to be present more and more as the head of the parish family. This means we should take care to integrate him as much as we can into normal weekly parish life. The temptation, of course, is to suspend normal parish life for the duration of his visit, so that we can concentrate on formal dinners and special ways of honoring him as an unusual guest. Normal parish life resumes only after he has gone. This is part of the problem. There is of course nothing wrong with formal dinners, but we also need the bishop to be present in the parish at its normal functions, not as an unusual guest but as our father.

That means we want him in our midst, not only holding a *trikerion* and *dikerion* in his hands at his hierarchical Divine Liturgy, but also afterward, holding a burger and drink in those hands at the parish picnic. That is how we experience the parish priest among us, and we need to experience the diocesan bishop in the same way as well. When the bishop comes, we may indeed greet him with the customary gifts of bread and salt, but normal parish activities should not be suspended during his visit. If we normally hold Sunday School before the Liturgy, we should continue to do so, and have him meet the children. If we normally have an inquirers' class afterward, we should still have it, and let him help field the inquirers' inquiries. We must learn to regard his presence not as an *interruption* of our parish life, but as its *normal basis*. There will still be plenty of time for formal dinners.

When our own bishop recently visited our little mission in Langley, B.C., and we were scuttling around getting everything ready for the hierarchical service ("Are the *trikeri* and *dikeri* lit? Where's his staff?"), we momentarily lost track of him. I am pleased to say we soon found him in the church library, surrounded by children, reading them a story—as if his episcopal presence were the most natural thing in the world. The children that day knew better than the subdeacons and I did. We regarded the bishop's presence as something gloriously unusual; the children regarded it as just another part of life at St. Herman's.

Secondly, we should invite the bishop to fulfill his historical and canonical role in sacramental initiations. In the pre-Nicene Church and even later, it was the bishop who presided at every baptism. Possibly ways could be found for him to preside now, perhaps by scheduling such baptisms/chrismations during his time in the parish. Baptism helps bind the newly initiated and their family to the priest who does the baptizing. Why should they not also have these precious connections with their bishop? In the same way, people may be encouraged to be anointed and prayed for by the bishop when he comes. The bishop's historical role was as the chief liturgizer in the church; the presbyters were those who counseled and assisted him in this role. We should come to the bishop now as often as possible, so that the hands that bless us in the Liturgy are also the hands that heal us in other sacramental encounters. God gives us bishops as conduits of healing and grace, and it is time we came once again to that healing source.

Thirdly, the faithful should be encouraged to come to the bishop for his pastoral advice and supporting prayers. We are always delighted to shake the bishop's hand and to take his blessing, but he has more to give than can be gained in such brief encounters. He has wisdom and experience as well (often many years of it), and two listening ears. If we have problems or burdens, we could well share them with our father-in-God, receive his counsel, and ask his prayers. That is, we could come to him as a true pastoral presence and let the Lord, the great Shepherd of the sheep (Heb. 13:20), work through him.

Fourthly, we should get to know him. When the bishop visits but rarely, it is hard to know him as a person. In fact, if we are honest, we often don't regard him as a real flesh-and-blood person at all, but solely as the bearer of episcopal dignity. Of course he retains his episcopal dignity, but before he is a bishop he is our brother in Christ, and like all our brothers, he has many stories to tell—stories that can benefit us. Do we really know him? Have we heard the stories of his life? If he came from a monastery, have we listened to his experiences as a young monk there? If he is a convert to the Orthodox Faith, have we heard the story of his conversion? All clergy have many stories to tell, stories which make them real to us as persons and which bind us to him as our pastor. We need these same treasured links with our bishop as well.

Too often, I suspect, we treat our bishops as Canadians treat their queen. That is, we don't really know her and would not presume to really get to know her if we could. If somehow introduced to the queen, we would never say, "How are you feeling, Your Majesty? Is your day going well? Have you seen William and Kate and the new baby lately?" We would never presume to have a real relationship; rather, we would remain silent until spoken to and then mostly just bow or curtsey. For us, Elizabeth II is not a real person in the same way the other people in our parish are real people. For us she is mostly just Her Majesty the Queen. It is important that we don't regard the bishop in the same way, as simply His Grace the Bishop, as a two-dimensional figure of authority. Under the miter is a real flesh-and-blood man of God; underneath the sakkos beats the heart of a brother in Christ. We will be enriched if we can get to know him, open ourselves up to him, and let him get to know us in turn.

Finally, we should pray for him, and not just in our weekly Divine Liturgy and in the services, but every day in our private prayers. We pray daily for our parish priest (or we should); let us pray for our bishop as well. He certainly needs our prayers. As a bishop, he will have to bear burdens and face challenges we can know little of. All the more reason to hold him in our hearts and to hold him up in prayer every day before God.

This volume opened with the vision of an empty throne, the bishop's chair in the parish church on which he hardly ever sits. Bishops are a tremendous gift to the Church; they are the fountain from which all sacramental grace proceeds, and theirs is the confession of Orthodoxy on which the local church is built. For this alone we owe them a tremendous debt of gratitude in Christ. Our aim and our joy is to have them in our midst as often as possible, filling their thrones and blessing us, their children.

For Further Reading

Afanasiev, Nicholas, *The Church of the Holy Spirit* (Notre Dame: University of Notre Dame Press, 2007).

Larin, Vassa, *The Byzantine Hierarchal Divine Liturgy in Arsenij Suxanov's Proskinitarij* (Rome: Pontificio Istituto Orientale, 2010).

Michalopulos, George, and Herb Ham, *The American Orthodox Church: A History of Its Beginnings* (Salisbury, MA, Regina Press, 2003).

Rapp, Claudia, *Holy Bishops in Late Antiquity* (Berkeley: University of California Press, 2005).

Zizioulas, John D., *Eucharist, Bishop, Church* (Brookline: Holy Cross Press, 2001).

We hope you have enjoyed and benefited from this book. Your financial support makes it possible to continue our non-profit ministry both in print and online. Because the proceeds from our book sales only partially cover the costs of operating **Ancient Faith Publishing** and **Ancient Faith Radio**, we greatly appreciate the generosity of our readers and listeners. Donations are tax-deductible and can be made at **www.ancientfaith.com.**

To view our other publications,
please visit our website: **store.ancientfaith.com**

Bringing you Orthodox Christian music, readings,
prayers, teaching, and podcasts 24 hours a day since 2004 at
www.ancientfaith.com

www.ingramcontent.com/pod-product-compliance
Lightning Source LLC
Chambersburg PA
CBHW071735080526
44588CB00013B/2042